A COLLAB[...]

PAMELA MANTEY

AND BUSINESS THOUGHT LEADERS & SUCCESS STRATEGISTS

IT TAKES
MONEY
Honey

Guaranteed Strategies to Wealth Creation, Proven Tips for Financial Freedom & Developing Faith

CONTENTS

DEDICATION

To all women who have boldly embraced the life of freedom, faith and leveling up in their finances. For those shifting into position to Live the Life they dream of - this is for you!

PREFACE

For decades, women have transcended and paved a way for other women. It is said that success leaves clues. The short cut to success is learning and gleaning from others who have been where you are going. The key to exposure and visibility is in the power of collaboration. Together we succeed. This compilation of spiritual entrepreneurs, women of influence and thought leaders will elevate, educate, equip and inspire you to overcome challenges and break through limitations. This inspirational journal book is to be digested daily to prepare your mind and spirit to win each day. Write down any thoughts, ideas and revelations that come to you. Let this work undergird your daily responses to circumstances.

ABOUT THE VISIONARY

Pamela Mantey is a Life Coach and a Wealth Builder who creates incubators to nurture women in the right moral atmosphere for the effective development of their purpose and passion. She teaches unique and proven entrepreneurial concepts to turn your ideas and gifts into wealth making ventures. She is a powerful conference speaker and mentor to women around the globe. Pamela Mantey overcame significant health challenges which has evoked her extraordinary passion for living life purposefully and with intention. She is known for taking women on her journey of empowerment and transformation to become who they are called to be.

Pamela Mantey is the Founder of GLOW Women's Network, a spiritual hub with resources to help women birth their God given purpose. She is also the CEO of It Takes Money Honey Network, an events and media platform, interviewing and engaging successful entrepreneurs and small business owners in inspirational and educational conversations. She provides her clients with exposure and expansion of their brands, while teaching and equipping her audience with relevant strategies and techniques to have successful businesses.

Pamela Mantey is the author of "Fulfilled: Five Keys to Achieve Your Dreams" and soon to be released, "Simply Irresistible Wife" and "Simply Irresistible Single Woman" books.

ACKNOWLEDGMENTS

This book collaboration has taken me on a journey to connect with some remarkable women who are impacting lives globally. I'm humbled to be in your company, Queens. Each and everyone of you are special, indeed. Your immense support has made this project the success that it is. Together, we are changing lives one day at a time.

REVIEWS

"As I read excerpts from this book, I am struck by the amazing stories of pain, strength and victory. It is clear that when these women put their mind, body and soul in "it," they can accomplish the very thing others said they could never do! These women have learned, through grace and grit, that no one and nothing can defeat you!" (Luke 22:32)

LaTanya Johnson

First Lady of Apostles Doctrine Ministry, Chesterfield, VA and Lieutenant, Department of Corrections

latanyajohnson1099@gmail.com

"What an insightful and thought-provoking collaboration! These ladies are offering a deeper understanding in their area of expertise to encourage a growth mindset to learn, overcome obstacles and rise. Excellent!

Andrea Holman

Singer.Songwriter.Storyteller

http://www.andreaholman.com/

DAY 1 – A FRESH START

"Therefore, if anyone is in Christ, the new creation has come: The old has gone, the new is here." - 1 Corinthians 5:17

Everyone loves a new beginning, a fresh start, a second chance to live the life you have always dreamed of. A chance to right the wrongs, correct your mistakes to rise above any regrets to a better future. Today, you have been given the gift of a blank page to be the author of your own story and destiny. Today, the old has passed away and all things are new.

_____

_____

_____

ABOUT THE AUTHOR

Pamela Mantey is the President of GLOW Women's Network which is a spiritual hub with resources to help women birth their God given purpose.
Pamela Mantey
www.glownetwork.org
https://www.facebook.com/GlowWomensNetwork/
https://www.facebook.com/groups/GLOWWOMENSNETWORK/?ref=share
Pam@glownetwork.org

DAY 2 – NEW YEAR, NEW YOU

"The definition of insanity is doing the same thing over and over and expecting different results." - Albert Einstein

To be honest with you, a new year does not depict a new you. A day crossing through the night to a new year doesn't mean things have changed. As long as your mindset, attitude and perception are the same, nothing truly changes. Real change begins with your mindset. It is said that insanity is doing the same thing and expecting a different result. You must set your mind free by open mindedness to experience an extraordinary life.

_____

_____

_____

ABOUT THE AUTHOR

Pamela Mantey is the President of GLOW Women's Network which is a spiritual hub with resources to help women birth their God given purpose.
Pamela Mantey
www.glownetwork.org
https://www.facebook.com/GlowWomensNetwork/
https://www.facebook.com/groups/GLOWWOMENSNETWORK/?ref=share
Pam@glownetwork.org

DAY 3 – SURRENDER TO HIS PROCESS

"And Jesus answered and said unto him, What wilt thou that I should do unto thee? The blind man said unto him, Lord, that I might receive my sight." - Mark 10:51

The blind man screamed and yelled to draw Jesus' attention.

Jesus came and asked him surprisingly what he can do to him and not for him. Most of the time you expect Him to do for you. He wants to do 'to' you. He strengthens, empowers, transforms and takes you through the process so that you can rise up to walk the path of your calling. Allow Him to continue His work in you!

_____

_____

_____

ABOUT THE AUTHOR

Pamela Mantey is the President of GLOW Women's Network which is a spiritual hub with resources to help women birth their God given purpose.
Pamela Mantey
www.glownetwork.org
https://www.facebook.com/GlowWomensNetwork/
https://www.facebook.com/groups/GLOWWOMENSNETWORK/?ref=share
Pam@glownetwork.org

DAY 4 – ATTRACTION TO MANIFESTATION

"For as he thinketh in his heart, so is he" - Proverbs 23:7

Transformation starts from within. Your affirmations are not just what you say but your deep-seated beliefs. You can speak of abundance, success, and prosperity but if your deep-seated beliefs are of fear, doubt and rejection that is what you will inevitably attract. Therefore, begin to pay attention to your inner vibrations. As you speak let your inner beliefs shine through by eliminating all negativity. You will begin to attract what you really desire.

_____

_____

_____

ABOUT THE AUTHOR

Pamela Mantey is the President of GLOW Women's Network which is a spiritual hub with resources to help women birth their God given purpose.
Pamela Mantey
www.glownetwork.org
https://www.facebook.com/GlowWomensNetwork/
https://www.facebook.com/groups/GLOWWOMENSNETWORK/?ref=share
Pam@glownetwork.org

DAY 5 – HAVE A CLEAR VISION

"Achieving your vision doesn't mean you've reached the end of the line. It simply means that you've come to a new starting place." - Nido Qubein

It is impossible accomplish anything worth having, without a vision. A vision is a clear and graphic image of your dreams; a vivid imagination or concept of your future. God is a God of vision and He created us to operate in the same manner. Do you have a clear direction for your life this year? Where do you see your life by the end of the year. Reverse engineer your vision, create goals to achieve them.

_____

_____

_____

ABOUT THE AUTHOR

Pamela Mantey is the President of GLOW Women's Network which is a spiritual hub with resources to help women birth their God given purpose.
Pamela Mantey
www.glownetwork.org
https://www.facebook.com/GlowWomensNetwork/
https://www.facebook.com/groups/GLOWWOMENSNETWORK/?ref=share
Pam@glownetwork.org

DAY 6 – TOTAL LIFE SUCCESS

"Success is simple. Do what's right, the right way, at the right time." - Arnold H. Glasgow

Total life success encompasses every area of your life. Your Personal Life, Business/Career, Relationships, Spiritual Life, Financial, Mind/Intellect, and Health. Zig Ziglar calls it the "wheel of life." You cannot look at these areas of life in isolation when it comes to success. Unless you are successful in all, you are missing true success . Your vision, dreams, goals and its implementation has to include all these core areas of your life. Create your wheel of life today.

_____

_____

_____

ABOUT THE AUTHOR

Pamela Mantey is the President of GLOW Women's Network which is a spiritual hub with resources to help women birth their God given purpose.
Pamela Mantey
www.glownetwork.org
https://www.facebook.com/GlowWomensNetwork/
https://www.facebook.com/groups/GLOWWOMENSNETWORK/?ref=share
Pam@glownetwork.org

DAY 7 — MASTER YOUR GOALS

"If the ladder is not leaning against the right wall, every step we take just gets us to the wrong place faster." - Stephen R. Covey

There are many who climb the ladder all the way to the top only to realize their ladder is on the wrong wall. You have to set goals that align with your purpose and destiny. Those are your Master Goals. If your goals are not aligned, there not be any fulfillment in your achievement. Do not be distracted by (SOS) Shiny Object Syndrome. Be focused and steadfast in your lane, your vision and your dreams in front of you.

_____

_____

_____

ABOUT THE AUTHOR

Pamela Mantey is the President of GLOW Women's Network which is a spiritual hub with resources to help women birth their God given purpose.
Pamela Mantey
www.glownetwork.org
https://www.facebook.com/GlowWomensNetwork/
https://www.facebook.com/groups/GLOWWOMENSNETWORK/?ref=share
Pam@glownetwork.org

DAY 8 – EMBRACE THE GRACE OF AGED WOMEN

"Here am I, send me." - Abraham 3:27

To live is with love, hope, determination and praying for all mankind. Seek wisdom from women of age, whose heart, and message of knowledge, will empower your dreams.

"Keep Winning; Stay Faithful," says Mamie. "With Jehovah God, whatever your heart's desire is yours," says Burnese.

"Be Nice, Be Kind, Be Gentle" say's Freddie Lee

"Trust Him," as I reflect on my grandmother's words of wisdom, I feel their warmth and direction each day.

_____

_____

_____

ABOUT THE AUTHOR

Candace L. Lynch-Wilkerson is originally from Augusta, Georgia and currently live in Rockville, Maryland. She operates out of the wisdom of the aged women in her life everyday.
candacewilkerson94@gmail.com

DAY 9 – SERVE GOD FIRST

"For the love of money is a root of all kinds of evil,". -1 Timothy 6:10a (NKJV)

Some believe that money is evil; that is untrue. The biblical truth is: "loving money" above God is evil, because we are to "worship no other gods before Him". We worship something when we look to that thing or person to completely fulfill us. Do you worship money or God? The "love of money" is idolatry, which is worshipping a false god. Love God and use money to glorify Him.

_____

_____

_____

ABOUT THE AUTHOR

Rachel Leigh, MBA/ Author/ Speaker/ Coach
Jackson, Tennessee
RachelLeigh0180@gmail.com
Facebook page: Living Water Bible Studies
www.facebook.com/WarriorAngelMinistries

DAY 10 – GREAT GRACE

"And He said unto me, 'My grace is sufficient for you, for my strength is made perfect in weakness'." - 2 Corinthians 12:9a (NKJV)

He sees our every move and knows our every motive. We daily fail Him by falling short of His Glory. We have weaknesses we would rather hide than admit. Still, He loves us enough to show us His ever abiding and constantly renewing sweet, sweet Grace! He gracefully pardons our sins through the power and salvation provided through His Son. His Blessing of Grace is truly always and eternally enough!

_____

_____

_____

ABOUT THE AUTHOR

Rachel Leigh, MBA/ Author/ Speaker/ Coach
Jackson, Tennessee
RachelLeigh0180@gmail.com
Facebook page: Living Water Bible Studies
www.facebook.com/WarriorAngelMinistries

DAY 11 – MIGHTY MERCY

God's Mercies "are new every morning". - Lamentations 3:23a (NKJV)

We have eternal forgiveness as we remain and abide in Christ; we also have a refreshing starting point from which to draw on this promise. Each day. we are offered His merciful love and forgiveness over again. How sweet it is to taste the new mercy He serves each morning.

No matter how far we stray, there He awaits our return to Him. How precious and powerful is His Mercy!

_____

_____

_____

ABOUT THE AUTHOR

Rachel Leigh, MBA/ Author/ Speaker/ Coach
Jackson, Tennessee
RachelLeigh0180@gmail.com
Facebook page: Living Water Bible Studies
www.facebook.com/WarriorAngelMinistries

DAY 12 – FAITH AND POSITIVE MINDSET

Faith and Positive Mindset Scripture:

Let your light so shine before men, that they may see your good works, and glorify your Father which is in heaven. Matthew 5:16 King James Version (KJV).

It can be challenging to maintain your faith and positive mindset. Make a daily commitment to pray and meditate. This ensures, a pouring of positive energy into your spirit enabling a positive mindset, turn on your light, so that you may SHINE and touch the people around you. Remember like attracts like. Write down your thoughts every day. In the evening reflect on all the positive ways you've touched people as well as how they've touched you. Follow this with a prayer of thanksgiving, gratitude and pray for continued guidance and peace.

_____

_____

_____

ABOUT THE AUTHOR

April Mack-Williams
Author | Coach | Minister | Motivator
Cincinnati, Ohio
Email: TheAprilMackWilliams@gmail.com
www.facebook.com/TheAprilMackWilliams

DAY 13 – CHANGE YOUR MINDSET!

"I Can Do All Things through Christ Who Strengthens Me" (Philippians 4:13)

We often convince ourselves that certain goals are beyond our reach. For example, one person may say, "I will never get my dream job." Do you know why they never got their dream job? They simply talked themselves out of it and consequently missed their blessings.

Change your mindset, which starts inside of you.

_____

_____

_____

ABOUT THE AUTHOR

Lanee Smith is a magazine publisher and author who writes to inspire, empower and encourage women to become successful.
bayareamag@gmail.com
fb.me/laneeonline

DAY 14 – REVERENT IN RESISTANCE

> She bowed down with her face to the ground. She asked him, "Why have I found such favor in your eyes that you notice me a foreigner? (Ruth 2:10).

Like Ruth, many of us went through deep pain, loss, and resistance from the closest people we love. Feelings of rejection make you want to run, yet God´s redemptive love and kindness lead you to rest in reverence. The kindness of Boaz helped Ruth trust and feel safe in his field, allowing the past pain to melt in his reverent example. Being reverent helps you to rest rather than run.

_____

_____

_____

ABOUT THE AUTHOR

Rev. Treneta Bowden is the president of FAM, John Maxwell speaker, coach and trainer, singer, award winning songwriter bringing faith, hope and healing to precious lives everywhere.
www.Trenetasong.com
www.Honormarriage.com
www.Faitharise.com

DAY 15 – TRUST GOD'S COVENANT PROMISE

"I will maintain my love for him forever and my covenant with him will never fail." - Psalm 89:28

When God speaks to us, we can trust him at His word. Doubts may steal the word that was sown, but you can know our God is on the throne. Storms of life and silence of the unseen may steal what you have heard. You can know, precious one, God will never violate his love or word. Abraham waited patiently and received what was promised. So shall you also receive (Heb. 6:15).

_____

_____

_____

ABOUT THE AUTHOR

Rev. Treneta Bowden is the president of FAM, John Maxwell speaker, coach and trainer, singer, award winning songwriter bringing faith, hope and healing to precious lives everywhere.

www.Trenetasong.com
www.Honormarriage.com
www.Faitharise.com

DAY 16 – FREEDOM IN KNOWING

"I will walk about in freedom, for I have sought out your precepts." - Psalm 119:45

Knowing Who Jesus is, what He has already done and who you are in Him, is freedom. Let's talk about getting to know Jesus. How do you get to know anyone? You spend time with them, you make time for them, and you talk with them. Jesus is real. And He desires communication with you. So, read, meditate and pray God's Word.

_____

_____

_____

ABOUT THE AUTHOR

Deidra is a faith talking, freedom walking, take God at His Word woman who does not back down in the face of adversity.
Deidra Pittman
Tampa, Florida
www.taxeivas.com
https://www.facebook.com/taxdeivas/

DAY 17 – BECOMING THE BEST ME

> "What makes believers different from the rest of the world is our ability to get back up when we fall down." - Alandes Powell

Really God, you love me this much? The next pages are strategies I used to keep my faith during hopeless times and increase my finances when the math didn't add up.

_____

_____

_____

ABOUT THE AUTHOR

Alandes is Board Chair of GSW-Ohio Urban League and Elder Board member of megachurch, Inspiration Bible. She has served on several non-profit boards and is committed to driving equality and self-sufficiency with people. She has received several awards, most notably: YWCA Career Woman and Cincinnati Enquirer/Greater Cincinnati Foundation Woman of the Year. She is a motivational speaker, expert in Operational Leadership with over 30 years in the financial industry. Alandes and her husband, Gordon have 4 children and 4 grandchildren.
Alandes Powell
Cincinnati, Ohio
www.facebook.com/AlandesPowell
www.instagram/@Alandesp

DAY 18 – PRIORITIZING LIFE

"We must prioritize how we will approach our life in order to realize when we step out of bounds." - Alandes Powell

Faith – I believe in the Father, His son Jesus and the Holy Spirit that surrounds us.

Family – My heart beats for the ones I love. At the end of my earthly days, it will be my family that will be impacted, not my career, but those who have loved me. So, I love hard and forgive fast.

Finances – Wealth is always right around the corner as long as we remain great stewards of what we have received. You reap what You sow.

For me, it's simple: Faith, Family & Finances

_____

_____

ABOUT THE AUTHOR

Alandes is Board Chair of GSW-Ohio Urban League and Elder Board member of megachurch, Inspiration Bible. She has served on several non-profit boards and is committed to driving equality and self-sufficiency with people. She has received several awards, most notably: YWCA Career Woman and Cincinnati Enquirer/Greater Cincinnati Foundation Woman of the Year. She is a motivational speaker, expert in Operational Leadership with over 30 years in the financial industry. Alandes and her husband, Gordon have 4 children and 4 grandchildren.
Alandes Powell
Cincinnati, Ohio
www.facebook.com/AlandesPowell
www.instagram/@Alandesp

DAY 19 — POWER OF FAITH

> "I get my super power from my faith and I maintain my faith by staying prayed up." - Alandes Powell

When pastors mention tithing people quickly say, "There he goes again pleading for money." When actually pastors are teaching how to increase prosperity and abundance even when the math doesn't work. They are teaching how to experience joy during both the bad and good times.

Tithing is an act of faith that ignites supernatural stretching of our dollar and moves mountains on our behalf. It is based on the divine principle that all we have comes from God and belongs to God.

Some say they can't afford to tithe, I say you can't afford not to.

ABOUT THE AUTHOR

Alandes Powell
Cincinnati, Ohio
www.facebook.com/AlandesPowell
www.instagram/@Alandesp

DAY 20 – WHERE ARE THOSE SHOES?

"The person who doesn't know where his next dollar is coming from usually doesn't know where his last dollar went." - Unknown

We get excited when they arrive; we count their toes and think about all we want for their lives. We can't wait to purchase their first pair of Jordans, and smile as we put the too big shoe on their tiny little feet.

Our need to impress others takes us from a "family wealth" model to a "isn't his outfit cute" model. We fail to invest in their financial future.

Just think if we would have invested in Nike Stock instead of buying Nike shoes what our child's financial portfolio may have included.

_____

_____

_____

ABOUT THE AUTHOR

Alandes Powell
Cincinnati, Ohio
www.facebook.com/AlandesPowell
www.instagram/@Alandesp

DAY 21 – WHAT DO YOU BELIEVE?

"What keeps me free isn't my money, it's my principles"

- Alandes Powell

I believe:

- It all, from Genesis to Revelations, I believe.

- The only person I am better than is the me from yesterday.

- I could easily be the person begging on the street so I look into their eyes, say hello, give them what I can muster up in money and say a prayer.

- Loving yourself is what makes it easy to love others.

- The greatest gift we have is kindness.

- We use money to impress others who aren't worth impressing.

ABOUT THE AUTHOR

Alandes Powell
Cincinnati, Ohio
www.facebook.com/AlandesPowell
www.instagram/@Alandesp

DAY 22 – ARE MONEY STRATEGIES REALLY PRACTICAL?

"Money is like a diet, we know what to do but doing it becomes the problem. Before you know it, you have eaten too many calories and spent too much money."

- Alandes Powell

As you can see below, money strategies are simple to list, but hard to follow. We use money for artificial happiness or to impress people who aren't worth impressing.

Legally Make Money	7.6 million people are considered "working poor"
Save	63% have less than $500.00 saved
Maintain Good Credit	Average score is fair 687
Keep a Budget	32% maintain a budget
Invest	54% of Americans invest in stock, but 92% of the stocks are owned by the wealthy

Maybe we should just agree to do better tomorrow.

_____

_____

_____

ABOUT THE AUTHOR

Alandes Powell
Cincinnati, Ohio
www.facebook.com/AlandesPowell
www.instagram/@Alandesp

DAY 23 — MAKING MONEY

"If a man will not work, he shall not eat." - 2 Thessalonians 3:10

I love the quote "Choose a job you love and never work a day in your life." It's true, but something that many of us will never experience. I would venture to guess the lion share of us work to get paid.

Finding a career that aligns to our skills can be stressful but something we all have to do if we don't want to "work a day in our lives."

Helpful Hints: Pray, remember declines aren't personal, passion in your job search helps, use your network and the network of others and get resume help

You got this!

_____

_____

_____

ABOUT THE AUTHOR

Alandes Powell
Cincinnati, Ohio
www.facebook.com/AlandesPowell
www.instagram/@Alandesp

DAY 24 – I KEEP TRYING TO SAVE

"Do not save what is left after spending, but spend what is left after saving." - Warren Buffett

Have you ever noticed that whenever you decide to save, something happens? I remember saving and suddenly my car broke down. I complained to my dad who said, "At least you had the money to fix it." True, but once you use your savings, it is difficult to get started again. However I have found accepting challenges to be helpful. Here's one:

Try the $5.00 Challenge!

Pay using cash (except gas I'm lazy).

Every $5.00 bill you receive has to be saved.

One year later, count it and invest it; I like the ACORN app.

You will never look at $5.00 Bills the same!

_____

_____

_____

ABOUT THE AUTHOR

Alandes Powell
Cincinnati, Ohio
www.facebook.com/AlandesPowell
www.instagram/@Alandesp

DAY 25 – WHY IS MY SCORE SO LOW?

"The only person you should worry about what they say behind your back is the credit bureau." - Alandes Powell

Credit reports are, at times, both a pain and a lifesaver. The better the credit score the lower the interest rate. Trying to figure out the score calculation can be challenging, however following these basic rules should help.

- Know what's on your report and who reported to the Credit Bureau.

- Always pay bills reported before reaching 30 days late. (Cell & Utilities normally do not report)

- It is better to use several cards and stay 30% under the credit limit.

- Never close an account that you have paid in full, unless they charge an annual fee.

_____

_____

_____

ABOUT THE AUTHOR

Alandes Powell
Cincinnati, Ohio
www.facebook.com/AlandesPowell
www.instagram/@Alandesp

DAY 26 – WHAT'S IN YOUR WALLET?

"May the budget odds be ever in your favor." - Alandes Powell

A friend decided to work three jobs because of being strapped with bills. He was stressed and when I asked him how much he was short each month, he had zero clue. He was what I call, "Financially Running Still."

In order to take the right action, you must know your current situation. Like dieting, we get on the scale first and then start planning.

Make it simple at first, grab a notepad and just list your income compared to bills. You can expand from there but the first step is critical.

_____

_____

_____

ABOUT THE AUTHOR

Alandes Powell
Cincinnati, Ohio
www.facebook.com/AlandesPowell
www.instagram/@Alandesp

DAY 27 — THE ZERO MONEY CHALLENGE

"Taking the emotions out of spending is the first step to changing our financial position." - Alandes Powell

A 26-year old man started the "Zero Day Challenge" and in six months he was able to save $18,432. The goal is to have as many zero days as you can each week. The only money you can spend without counting against you are already established bills. FYI, gas and food are not established bills.

You will need to track your spending, remember only about 32% of Americans have enough discipline to do this, and find another person to help hold you accountable.

Let's do this.

_____

_____

_____

ABOUT THE AUTHOR

Alandes Powell
Cincinnati, Ohio
www.facebook.com/AlandesPowell
www.instagram/@Alandesp

DAY 28 – A PRAYER FOR YOU

"When I talk to Him he listens, he never judges and always forgives." - Alandes Powell

Father, I pray and ask you to go before the person reading this and bless every aspect of their life. Forgive all their trespasses and provide them with the peace in Philippians 4:7, which surpasses all understanding. As they give, I pray it will be given to them according to your word in Luke 6:38. I pray they find joy on their journey and declare blessing over their family, their health and their finances. I pray in the name of the Father, the Son & the Holy Spirit.

Amen

_____
_____
_____

ABOUT THE AUTHOR

Alandes Powell
Cincinnati, Ohio
www.facebook.com/AlandesPowell
www.instagram/@Alandesp

DAY 29 – BITTER OR BETTER

"In everything give thanks: for this is the will of God in Christ Jesus concerning you." -

1 Thessalonians 5:18 (KJV)

Our response to adversity and obstacles in life is our choice. We can choose to be better, humbling ourselves before God, forgiving others, and being grateful for what we have; or we can choose to allow the things we experience to make us bitter. Before choosing to give up or keep going, remember the joy of the Lord is our strength and God's strength is never limited by our circumstances.

_____

_____

_____

ABOUT THE AUTHOR

ShaNita Nolan is a soul on fire for Christ, author, empowerment speaker, coach, trainer, and seasoned leadership and professional development expert.
ShaNita Nolan
Author, Speaker, Coach, & Trainer

DAY 30 – GOD'S INDESTRUCTIBLE PROMISE

"For I know the plans ai have for you, declares the Lord, plans for welfare and not for evil, to give you a future and a hope." Jeremiah 29:11 (ESV)

The fact that God chose us and created us to glorify Him, while we gave Him nothing should humble us. Whatever we may be faced with today or tomorrow, God has promised to be with us, even until the end of the world. This is His promise and it is greater than any pain that we will ever experience.

_____

_____

_____

ABOUT THE AUTHOR

ShaNita Nolan is a soul on fire for Christ, author, empowerment speaker, coach, trainer, and seasoned leadership and professional development expert.
ShaNita Nolan
Author, Speaker, Coach, & Trainer

DAY 31 – MANTLED FOR SUCCESS AND CREATED TO PROSPER

"Beloved, I wish above all things that thou mayest prosper and be in health, even as thy soul prospereth." - (KJV) 3 John 1:2

God's desire for us is to have the best life possible. His purpose for us is to live an abundant life. Prosperity and success are a part of our kingdom heritage that has been preordained for us. Proof of a kingdom mindset is when our will is in agreement with God's will. Here is where, our life begins to shift and align with our destiny, causing us to advance.

_____

_____

_____

ABOUT THE AUTHOR

Governing Apostle of For His Glory International-Chicago-Africa and Asia, Doctoral Degree in Divinity, CEO of GIFH and Owner of Anderson Tax and Finance
Apostle Dr. Sheila E. Anderson
Chicago, Illinois
www.iforhisglory.org
www.facebook.com/apostlesheila.anderson
www.facebook.com/iforhisglory/

DAY 32 – THERE IS ONLY ONE YOU – OWN IT

"I will praise thee; for I am fearfully *and* wonderfully made: marvelous *are* thy works; and *that* my soul knoweth right well." - Psalm 139:14 (KJV)

We were all made in the image and likeness of Christ, yet we are an original masterpiece. There is no one on this earth like you. The gifts you possess are specifically designed by God, for you. There are people only you can reach and touch with your life and testimony. Be the best version of yourself and God's best for you will follow.

_____

_____

_____

ABOUT THE AUTHOR

Governing Apostle of For His Glory International-Chicago-Africa and Asia, Doctoral Degree in Divinity, CEO of GIFH and Owner of Anderson Tax and Finance
Apostle Dr. Sheila E. Anderson
Chicago, Illinois
www.iforhisglory.org
www.facebook.com/apostlesheila.anderson
www.facebook.com/iforhisglory/

DAY 33 – NURTURE YOURSELF

"Women have purpose, power, and love that is needed to better serve the masses. We must strive to be our best self before taking on the world." - Renata Belgrave

Sugarfoots,
There will be times you will feel overwhelmed being a business woman, wife, or mom. Don't continue to pour from an empty cup. How are you going to refuel?

Take the time and focus on your spiritual health and wellness. Meditate on the word, so you can develop a strong relationship with God. This will give you a peace of mind and help you maintain a balanced and productive lifestyle.

_____

_____

_____

ABOUT THE AUTHOR

An author of Medical Records Tracker. A wife, mother, and Navy Veteran committed to creating lasting change in women's wellness.
Renata Belgrave
Jacksonville, Florida
www.loveintowellness.com
info@loveintowellness.com
https://www.facebook.com/renata.bel.50
amazon.com/author/renatabelgrave

DAY 34 – FINDING THE LIFE YOU LOVE

"Let Faith be your encourager and the foundation, now walk in your purpose."
- Renata Belgrave

Sugarfoots,

Have you ever felt unhappy or unmotivated waking up?

The problem is you are just existing, and not living life purposefully. It's time to grab some tea, pen, and your favorite notebook and do a self-evaluation in all areas of your life. Pray and ask God for guidance for a better understanding of what it is you were called to do, be specific. For more inspiration and support visit

www.loveintowellness.com.

_____

_____

_____

ABOUT THE AUTHOR

An author of Medical Records Tracker. A wife, mother, and Navy Veteran committed to creating lasting change in women's wellness.
Renata Belgrave
Jacksonville, Florida
www.loveintowellness.com
info@loveintowellness.com
https://www.facebook.com/renata.bel.50
amazon.com/author/renatabelgrave

DAY 35 — FAITH

"A combination of prayer, faith and action is needed when you come face to face with life challenges." - Renata Belgrave

Sugarfoots,

There will be things that happen in your life that you will not have control over. Don't give up! Start developing a faith mindset and have intimate conversations with God during hard times to get you through. This will give you the strength to be better equipped with obstacles that may come your way. Thank God for all your blessings, even when things are not going as planned. Remain faithful.

_____

_____

_____

ABOUT THE AUTHOR

An author of Medical Records Tracker. A wife, mother, and Navy Veteran committed to creating lasting change in women's wellness.
Renata Belgrave
Jacksonville, Florida
www.loveintowellness.com
info@loveintowellness.com
https://www.facebook.com/renata.bel.50
amazon.com/author/renatabelgrave

DAY 36 – FREEDOM

"How you treat yourself today will determine how you feel tomorrow." - Renata Belgrave

Sugarfoots,

If you don't develop self-love and practice self-care, it's impossible to have the freedom to live a healthy lifestyle. Fall in love with yourself and feed your mind with positivity and watch your life continue to change. You will have the freedom to live well, build healthy relationships with others, and gain the confidence to have financial freedom in your life. There is joy in knowing what you are capable of.

_____

_____

_____

ABOUT THE AUTHOR

An author of Medical Records Tracker. A wife, mother, and Navy Veteran committed to creating lasting change in women's wellness.
Renata Belgrave
Jacksonville, Florida
www.loveintowellness.com
info@loveintowellness.com
https://www.facebook.com/renata.bel.50
amazon.com/author/renatabelgrave

DAY 37 – FREEDOM

"If you will live like no one else, later you can live like no one else." - Dave Ramsey

Lack of self-discipline and economic status are the main reasons why many people remain in financial debt. Start planning your money rather than spending it; assess needs verses material desires. Financial freedom isn't about being rich. It's about having freedom to choose what to do with your money and not being weighed down by debt. Learn more about planning your money or even starting a small business.

_____

_____

_____

ABOUT THE AUTHOR

God First | Family | Servant Leader| Mentor| Small Business Consultant | Motivational Speaker| Visionary | Results Driven Professional
Tashawna Thomas Otabil
Cincinnati, Ohio
www.tashawnaotabilconsulting.com
TashawnaOtabil@gmail.com
www.facebook.com/TashawnaAnn

DAY 38 – RESILIENCE DRIVES EVOLUTION

"My purpose is far greater than my pain."- Foxy Brown

Everything changes and ends. Relationships, employment, health and wealth do not always go according to plan. Pain is part of life but so is your purpose. Discover the lessons contained within those experiences and you will evolve. You define your future and the next chapter will unfold according to your choices. Use your expertise to create a strategic growth plan to help you evolve.

_____

_____

_____

ABOUT THE AUTHOR

God First | Family | Servant Leader| Mentor| Small Business Consultant | Motivational Speaker| Visionary | Results Driven Professional
Tashawna Thomas Otabil
Cincinnati, Ohio
www.tashawnaotabilconsulting.com
TashawnaOtabil@gmail.com
www.facebook.com/TashawnaAnn

DAY 39 – CHOOSE TO BE FREE

"For to be free is not merely to cast off one's chains, but to live in a way that respects and enhances the freedom of others." - Nelson Mandela

I quit getting worked up over people and things I cannot change. I quit trying to gain approval. I quit internalizing opinions. I quit letting others hurt me. I quit expecting apologies. I quit being stressed. I quit pretending that my life is fine. I choose to have faith. I choose be grateful. I choose to be positive. I choose to have peace. I choose to protect my space. I choose to improve my life daily. I choose freedom.

_____

_____

_____

ABOUT THE AUTHOR

God First | Family | Servant Leader| Mentor| Small Business Consultant | Motivational Speaker| Visionary | Results Driven Professional
Tashawna Thomas Otabil
Cincinnati, Ohio
www.tashawnaotabilconsulting.com
TashawnaOtabil@gmail.com
www.facebook.com/TashawnaAnn

DAY 40 — JUST BELIEVE

"She is clothed with strength and dignity and she laughs without fear of the future." - Proverbs 31:25

You are strong. You are worthy. You are called. You will be anointed before you are positioned. All of your opportunities are wrapped in obedience. Stop trying to force things and figure out God's plans for you. Is the right man for me? Is that friendship really for me? Is that job opportunity really growing me? Cast your cares upon Him. God will move your heart and direct all your paths.

_____

_____

_____

ABOUT THE AUTHOR

God First | Family | Servant Leader| Mentor| Small Business Consultant | Motivational Speaker| Visionary | Results Driven Professional
Tashawna Thomas Otabil
Cincinnati, Ohio
www.tashawnaotabilconsulting.com
TashawnaOtabil@gmail.com
www.facebook.com/TashawnaAnn

DAY 41 – LIFE IS A JOURNEY

"The Journey will not be easy but worth it." – Tashawna Thomas Otabil

Life is a journey. There will be detours. Don't be discouraged. Detours provide knowledge and experiences that help transition you to the place you need to be. It's ok to get off at the exit to take a break, refuel your tank or perhaps feed your mind some positivity. Take time to deal with whatever it is that gets you off track AND then release it. Stop carrying baggage. You will eventually get back on track. Just remember that you are your greatest accomplishment, stay committed and believe in yourself.

_____

_____

_____

ABOUT THE AUTHOR

God First | Family | Servant Leader| Mentor| Small Business Consultant | Motivational Speaker| Visionary | Results Driven Professional
Tashawna Thomas Otabil
Cincinnati, Ohio
www.tashawnaotabilconsulting.com
TashawnaOtabil@gmail.com
www.facebook.com/TashawnaAnn

DAY 42 – YOU'RE IN CONTROL OF YOUR FINANCIAL FREEDOM

"Live on less than you make and don't owe people money" - Dave Ramsey

Learning to budget is a commitment, a process and a journey. It's similar to going on a weight loss journey. How many times have you tried to lose weight? Did you set realistic goals? Weight loss doesn't happen overnight and neither will changing your spending habits. If you want to be debt free, do what debt free people do. Stop buying STUFF. Pay off your debt. You don't have to be extreme, just consistent. Set small realistic achievable goals. Small changes equal to big results.

_____

_____

_____

ABOUT THE AUTHOR

God First | Family | Servant Leader| Mentor| Small Business Consultant | Motivational Speaker| Visionary | Results Driven Professional
Tashawna Thomas Otabil
Cincinnati, Ohio
www.tashawnaotabilconsulting.com
TashawnaOtabil@gmail.com
www.facebook.com/TashawnaAnn

DAY 43 — BE A PERSON OF VALUE

"Knowledge is of no value unless you put it into practice." -Anton Chekhov

How do you become more valuable? Do more. Pray more. Read more. Learn more. Give more. Be more. Serve more. Listen more. Travel more. Complain less. Judge less. Blame less. Worry Less. Gossip Less. Compare less. Hate less. Focus on your growth. Get rid of toxic behaviors. Be intentional about positive affirmations. Be committed to your own personal growth and development.

_____

_____

_____

ABOUT THE AUTHOR

God First | Family | Servant Leader| Mentor| Small Business Consultant | Motivational Speaker| Visionary | Results Driven Professional
Tashawna Thomas Otabil
Cincinnati, Ohio
www.tashawnaotabilconsulting.com
TashawnaOtabil@gmail.com
www.facebook.com/TashawnaAnn

DAY 44 – BE THE BEST VERSION OF YOURSELF

"I am in the process of becoming the best version of myself." - Tashawna Thomas Otabil

To have everything but nothing, to be an option rather than a choice, to fail at things that we most want to succeed at. To be used, unappreciated and taken for granted. We've all experienced similar emotions and encounters but do not let anyone determine your value. Push through and know your worth. Walk away from people and situations that threaten your peace. Surround yourself with people that see your value and remind you of it. You deserve the best version of yourself that comes from a deep knowing.

_____

_____

_____

ABOUT THE AUTHOR

God First | Family | Servant Leader| Mentor| Small Business Consultant | Motivational Speaker| Visionary | Results Driven Professional
Tashawna Thomas Otabil
Cincinnati, Ohio
www.tashawnaotabilconsulting.com
TashawnaOtabil@gmail.com
www.facebook.com/TashawnaAnn

DAY 45 – MOVING FORWARD WITH MOUNTAIN MOVING FAITH PART 1

"For whither thou goest, I will go; and where thou lodgest, I will lodge; thy people shall be my people, and thy God my God." - Ruth 1:16(b)KJV

Women of Faith, have you ever found yourself caught between a rock and a hard place? You know who the author and finisher of your faith is yet you are propelled into exercising your faith on a whole different level. You begin looking at your situation and secretly thinking that it seems impossible. Ruth didn't know what Naomi knew but she had to trust the process without having all the details. Ruth experienced many setbacks and disappointments..

_____

_____

_____

ABOUT THE AUTHOR

Cheryl D. Bryant is a wife, mother, preacher, teacher and the Co-Founder of Stephen & Cheryl Bryant Ministries in Dover, Deleware.
Contact us: scbministries14@gmail.com
www.facebook.com/@SCBMinistries
Write to us: PO Box 708 Felton, DE 19943

DAY 46 – MOVING FORWARD WITH MOUNTAIN MOVING FAITH PART 2

"For whither thou goest, I will go; and where thou lodgest, I will lodge; thy people shall be my people, and thy God my God." - Ruth 1:16(b)KJV

A famine had taken place in the land. Ruth was faced with the choice of moving to a place of uncertainty or staying where she was comfortable. We all will be faced with trusting God in our most uncomfortable seasons. Hold on ladies because you have mountain moving faith. Tap into the greatness and wealth on the inside. Declare the Word of God daily. Move Forward!

_____

_____

_____

ABOUT THE AUTHOR

Cheryl D. Bryant is a wife, mother, preacher, teacher and the Co-Founder of Stephen & Cheryl Bryant Ministries in Dover, Deleware.
Contact us: scbministries14@gmail.com
www.facebook.com/@SCBMinistries
Write to us: PO Box 708 Felton, DE 19943

DAY 47 — TITHING TO FINANCIAL ABUNDANCE

"Bring the whole tithe into the storehouse, that there may be food in my house. Test ME in this" says the Lord Almighty, "and see if I will not throw open the floodgates of heaven and pour out so much blessings that there will not be room enough to store it." - Malachi 3:10 (NIV)

It is true what they say, "Every time I tithe or gift I always end up with a little more money in my accounts than I had calculated. I see more blessings in my life!" The more you give away the more you will have! Can you imagine your life today having floodgates open up for you? What would you do? Take time to give thanks in a gratitude journal and connect with God in your daily quiet time; appreciate our Father's love and all He has done for us. Listen to the Holy Spirit telling us what we should do, which is not always what our worldly mind tells us to do. Make sure to keep that storehouse stocked and appreciate all the gifts in your life.

_____

_____

_____

ABOUT THE AUTHOR

Miriam M. Wright
Dream Life Coach/Network Marketing Consultant
Orlando, Florida
www.mmwdreams.com
livingyourdream@mmdreams.com
https://www.facebook.com/wrightwaytoyourdreams/

DAY 48 – YESTERDAY, TODAY & TOMORROW

Remember that "Yesterday is history, tomorrow is a mystery, but today is a gift that is why it is called the present". - Sun Dials and Roses of Yesterday: Garden Delights..." by Alice Morse Earle

Are you someone who lives in yesterdays? Are you someone who lives continually worrying about tomorrows? What about today? What are you planning to accomplish today? Remember this day is a gift to you; You woke up! That is the beginning of your blessings, Live each day like this moment is all there is and enjoy each moment to the fullest! Live in the here and now "present" and don't worry about the mystery of tomorrow. The Lord will be there to take care of you and all of your days.

_____

_____

_____

ABOUT THE AUTHOR

Miriam M. Wright
Dream Life Coach/Network Marketing Consultant
Orlando, Florida
www.mmwdreams.com
livingyourdream@mmdreams.com
https://www.facebook.com/wrightwaytoyourdreams/

DAY 49 – FROM FEAR TO FAITH

> "For assuredly, I say to you, whoever says to this mountain, 'Be removed and be cast into the sea,' and does not doubt in his heart, but believes that those things he says will be done, he will have whatever he says." - Mark 11:23

What is the obstacle in front of you that makes you fearful? How can you overcome it? Pray. Yes, but instead of saying "God, help me!" do what Jesus did: Speak to your mountain and tell it to go! Don't doubt! Hold on until you receive your answer. This is FAITH! When you trust Jesus and take Him at His Word, you can live the abundant life He promised you!

_____

_____

_____

ABOUT THE AUTHOR

Mary ScullyD wants to empower you to know your authority in Jesus, so that you can experience healing + hope.
Mary ScullyD
Wood-ridge, New Jersey
MaryScullyD@gmail.com
www.facebook.com/MaryScullyD

DAY 50 – THE UNSEEN FORTUNE

"Never be afraid to trust an unknown Future to a known GOD" -C.S. Lewis

The thing about faith is it can be born and it can die.

No one will actually have a measurement of faith as expected. The expansion of a woman's strength and vision within is more powerful than any living being. Greater is He that is inside us than he that is in the world. It's already won. It's already done. Live like every breathe is amazing

By the grace of God, I can testify that I'm still standing.

_____

_____

_____

ABOUT THE AUTHOR

Sandra Beverly Blushings
Springfield, Massachusetts
http://www.facebook.com/Beverly.cutpeopleoff

DAY 51 – WHO'S TO BLAME FOR YOUR CURRENT MONEY SITUATION?

"Stop Blaming Money! What is it that you're not creating? What is it that you're not choosing and what is it that you're not willing to receive about YOU?"

-Gary Douglas - Access Consciousness Founder

Taking time for self-care creates a well of energy within. When we have enthusiasm for life, we bring that same zest to our relationship with money. You can learn techniques and daily tools to relax and release what's locking you in personal and financial relationships.

_____

_____

_____

ABOUT THE AUTHOR

Kimberly Domke - Orlando FL
Kimberly shares techniques and daily tools to relax and release what's locking you in your personal and financial relationship. She uses the Energetic Touch aka the Access Consciousness Bars process, Aromatherapy and more.
FB : https://www.facebook.com/IntoMeISeeExperiences/

DAY 52 – FAITH, THE BRIDGE TO WHAT YOU WANT TO MANIFEST

"Faith is taking the first step, even when you don't see the whole staircase." - Martin Luther King, Jr.

A lot of people spend more time worrying about what they don't want instead of focusing on what they do want. Unfortunately, that misplacement of focus will only bring you more of what you don't want. Faith tunes you into and starts the divine flow that is already in you. The more faith you have, the quicker your request will be fulfilled.

_____

_____

_____

ABOUT THE AUTHOR

Janice Berkenheger
Professional Woman's Manifesting and Money Coach
https://www.facebook.com/JaniceBerkenheger
www.JaniceBerkenheger.com

DAY 53 – FROM CHAOS TO HARMONY: A SELF-CARE JOURNEY TOWARDS FREEDOM

"We need to take responsibility for our own health and wellness so that we can show up in our lives empowered, committed, authentic, and loving towards each other and our world." -Seane Corn

Stress can manifest in our body, mind, emotions and soul. Common stressors are muscle tension, worry, anxiety, and depression.

One of my favorite self-care practices is to massage oil into my body after a shower offering gratitude for all it has done. Gratitude conquers stress every time.

_____

_____

_____

ABOUT THE AUTHOR

Tracy is passionate about empowering women to fall in love with themselves with easy self-care rituals.
Tracy Rickard lives in Orlando, FL
@tracystotalwellness

DAY 54 — JUST KEEP MOVING!

"Have I not commanded you? Be strong and courageous. Do not be afraid; do not be discouraged, for the Lord your God will be with you wherever you go." Joshua 1:9 (NIV)

Once I was in a difficult situation and felt stuck, but God encouraged me to read Joshua 1:9. It was then that I realized that no matter what I decided or whichever way I went, as long as I leaned on God, He would always be there.

Now I take bold actions and I feel God's presence and see His hand wherever I go. Are you feeling stuck? Don't stall or procrastinate. Lean on Jesus and keep moving!

_____

_____

_____

ABOUT THE AUTHOR

Chou Hallegra
Dillsburg, Pennsylvania
https://www.facebook.com/ChouHallegra/

DAY 55 – FREE TO SEE

"Eyes that look are common; Eyes that see are rare"

- J. Oswald Sanders

However cliché, one thing leads to another. At the end of the day, the choice is yours. You can pick up those old blurry glasses... You know the ones I'm talking about.

The ones with the crack in one lens that you've been wearing so long that all the wiping in the world won't give you a clear view. Or, you can choose that new fancy pair that puts everything into perspective. Remember, you have a choice!

_____

_____

_____

ABOUT THE AUTHOR

CEO and Founder of Purpose Revealed NFP, an advocate for youth, she also writes short plays while serving the community.
Rocherr Landrum- Johnson
Chicago, Illinois
www.purposerevealed.org
www.facebook.com/revealedpurpose/

DAY 56 – PURPOSE REVEALED

"You can love me or hate me I swear it won't make me or break me" - Lil Wayne

Change your mind, Change your life! On your journey from victim to victor, focus less on the faults of others. Completely identify and seek healing for all those things that weigh you down and you will find your way. Find less fault in others and a peace that surpasses all understanding will effortlessly find you. In due time, your purpose will be revealed and you will find true freedom!

_____

_____

_____

ABOUT THE AUTHOR

CEO and Founder of Purpose Revealed NFP, an advocate for youth, she also writes short plays while serving the community.
Rocherr Landrum- Johnson
Chicago, Illinois
www.purposerevealed.org
www.facebook.com/revealedpurpose/

DAY 57 – JOURNEY TO HEALTHY

"Commit your work to the Lord, and your plans will be established." - Proverbs 16:3 ESV

Let's be honest. Weight loss is usually a selfish pursuit. We hope that God will bless our mundane efforts. However when we commit to our goals and invest in our health to Him, He will show up in a big way.

I tried every diet without success, Now I'm committed to keeping the weight off God's way.

_____

_____

_____

ABOUT THE AUTHOR

Rachel is determined to help you avoid making the same dieting mistakes while being focused on God.
Rachel Parrish
Oviedo, FL
www.MissPengwinFitness.com
Rachel@misspengwin.com
www.facebook.com/misspengwinfitness
www.instagram.com/misspengwinfitness

DAY 58 – BE YOUR OWN INSPIRATION

"Success is a daredevil that likes to jump onto moving trains. So get moving!" - Ella Glasgow

You've got a million lists to remind you of what you haven't done. Take time today to celebrate the wins. I call it the "Ya Did" List. It doesn't matter how small or how long ago. Write it ALL down. Even that time you learned to tie your shoes. And on days you begin to feel unaccomplished, take out your "Ya Did" List to remind yourself of all ya did!

_____

_____

_____

ABOUT THE AUTHOR

Ella Glasgow is a Vocal Impact Expert. After 20+ years as a professional vocalist, she's helping others command their stage and speak with confidence. Ella helps people create their "Ya Did" list.
Dallas, TX
www.yourvoicesuccess.com
ella@thevoicesuccesscoach.com
Twitter: @EllaGlasgow
www.facebook.com/EllaGlasgow

DAY 59 – SUCCESS IS A LONG-TERM GOAL

"Never take a no from someone who may not be in a position to give you a yes"
- Brandhyze Stanley

You already know this, but I'm going to remind you again. There is NO success (whatever that means to you) that happens overnight. NONE! Every success takes time. There are no shortcuts to doing the actual work. So stop making excuses for yourself about why you can't get things done. Be honest with yourself. Write it down right now and make a plan. Start with what you have on hand right now.

_____

_____

_____

ABOUT THE AUTHOR

Ella Glasgow is a Vocal Impact Expert. After 20+ years as a professional vocalist, she's helping others command their stage and speak with confidence. Ella helps people get clarity on your vision?
Dallas, TX
www.yourvoicesuccess.com
ella@thevoicesuccesscoach.com
Twitter: @EllaGlasgow
www.facebook.com/EllaGlasgow

DAY 60 — LIVING LIFE WITH VISION

"Age is whatever you think it is. You are as old as you think you are." - Muhammad Ali

"Think Young – Live Younger." That's our philosophy for creating a community of ageless living for men and women. Imagine a lifestyle that includes, mindset, nutrition, fitness, skin care, hair care, dress and grooming, and recreational fun regardless of your age. Imagine body care that includes natural plant-based approaches to disrupting the aging cycle and getting your energy and vitality back. Our community also offers solutions for thinning hair, aging skin, gut health, ramping up energy and mental vigor.

_____

_____

_____

ABOUT THE AUTHOR

Energetic, vibrant, wife, mother, grandmother, career corporate manager and entrepreneur as an Ageless Generation Strategist. Founder of Women's Entrepreneurial Empowerment.
Sabrina Protic
Brandon, Florida
www.agelesstechniques.com
www.wee-womenentrepreneurs.com
Facebook @AgelessTechniques (Page)
Facebook Sabrina Farmer (Protic)

DAY 61 – EMPOWER YOUR FEAR

"For me, becoming isn't about arriving somewhere or achieving a certain aim. I see it instead as forward motion, a means of evolving, a way to reach continuously toward a better self. The journey doesn't end." - Michelle Obama

Everyone's journey is different. Anxiety and fear may wake you up in the morning, follow you throughout the day and keep you up at night. You must step out on faith to face your fears and anxieties head on to live an intentional life and be empowered to moving forward. Ask yourself - Why am I afraid? What can I change right now? How can this help me better myself? Where do I start?

_____

_____

_____

ABOUT THE AUTHOR

Jaresha Moore is a qualified Success Coach who is passionate about helping people develop the skills and self-assurance they need to reach their potential.
Dayton, Ohio
www.empoweronpurpose.com
jaresha.moore@empoweronpurpose.com
www.facebook.com/Empoweronpurpose

DAY 62 – OVERCOME FEAR TO EMPOWER YOUR FREEDOM

"The other side of fear and anxiety is freedom. Freedom of fear will be yours only when you become brave and embrace your discomfort zone and be who God called you to be – strong women destined for greatness." - Jaresha Moore

Fears often keep us from being who God has called us to be. Overcoming fears of failure, being judged by others, or speaking in public will help you move from comfort to courage zone. You have to become aware of your fears, tell yourself the only way to overcome it is to face it. Just do it and celebrate all victories. The journey to freedom of fear begins with you being comfortably uncomfortable.

_____

_____

_____

ABOUT THE AUTHOR

Jaresha Moore is a qualified Success Coach who is passionate about helping people develop the skills and self-assurance they need to reach their potential.
Dayton, Ohio
www.empoweronpurpose.com
jaresha.moore@empoweronpurpose.com
www.facebook.com/Empoweronpurpose

DAY 63 – FAITH MORNINGS

> "Jesus said to him, 'If you can believe, all things *are* possible to him who believes.'" - Mark 9:23 (NKJV)

The bed covers say to me, "Stay in bed!" When I do, my day is busy but unproductive. There is not enough time to pray, study my bible, write my book or complete other daily goals.

Faith moves me from bed to action. Faith fuels my dreams. Rise early to perform actions for God's success in your life through your productivity.

_____

_____

_____

ABOUT THE AUTHOR

Annette is a believer, a speaker, and a paradigm shifting carepreneur devoted to doing good and living a productive life.
Annette Gayle
Orlando Florida
www.annetegayle.com
annette@annettegayle.com
www.facebook.com/annette.gayle.961

DAY 64 – SILENCE IS NOT ALWAYS GOLDEN

"One night the Lord spoke to Paul in a vision: "Do not be afraid; keep on speaking, do not be silent." - Acts 18:9 (NKJV)

Visions from God reassure us that He is with us. Many may not be ready to hear your message. It's okay. Have faith in your vision, don't betray it. Dr. Martin Luther King, Jr. said "A time comes when silence is betrayal".

Remember that your vision matters and it will make a positive difference in the world. The moment you begin to act on your vision is when your life truly begins, with purpose.

_____

_____

_____

ABOUT THE AUTHOR

Annette is a believer, a speaker, and a paradigm shifting carepreneur devoted to doing good and living a productive life.
Annette Gayle
Orlando Florida
www.annetegayle.com
annette@annettegayle.com
www.facebook.com/annette.gayle.961

DAY 65 – NEW MINDSET FOR LIFE AND FINANCIAL FREEDOM

"Positive thinking will let you do everything better than negative thinking will" - Zig Ziglar

Our lives are the accumulation of negative and positive thinking. Words are manifested thoughts which become our things. Therefore, thinking positive creates positive life experiences.

_____

_____

_____

ABOUT THE AUTHOR

Abundance Coach Sheila Willis started with a simple premise: help others to transform their lives in order to live their best lives yet. She earned a BA degree in Communications from Langston University in Langston Oklahoma. She's authored several eBooks on Amazon, and operates her Live from Your Heart and Mind website
Sheila Willis
San Diego, California
Certified Abundance Coach/Transformation Speaker/Author
www.lifecoachsheilawillis.com
bit.ly/shopselfhelpproducts
http://bit.ly/abundancecoachsheila
swillis@lifecoachsheilawillis.com

DAY 66 – SHIFT YOUR PERSPECTIVE TO INCREASE ABUNDANCE

"You can have anything you want when you give up the belief that you can't have it." - Sheila Willis

I often work with people who struggle with lack and scarcity despite their efforts to get ahead in life. Generally, the main reason for this is their mindset concerning abundance. The individuals that struggle in this area focus more on lack instead abundance. Since, what we focus on grows stronger more of the lack and scarcity that isn't wanted continues to show up. When they are taught to focus on what is desired rather than what's not in order to shift the mindset then positive results happen for them.

_____

_____

_____

ABOUT THE AUTHOR

Sheila Willis
San Diego, California
Certified Abundance Coach/Transformation Speaker/Author
www.lifecoachsheilawillis.com
bit.ly/shopselfhelpproducts
http://bit.ly/abundancecoachsheila
swillis@lifecoachsheilawillis.com

DAY 67 — A TRANSFORMED MIND YIELDS UNLIMITED ABUNDANCE

"All Things Are Possible to Them That Believe." Mark 9:23

Did you know that abundance, peace, and, well-being is a divine inheritance? However, due to many people's life experiences the natural state of abundance has been forgotten. The root cause of abundance problems are mindset issues. The mindsets of scarcity must be transformed for lasting abundance. Mindset issues deal with our relationship to money. Because, mindset issues are happening at a subconscious level many attempt to change external things fail while the real issue remains internal. Permanent change only occurs with an internal change this then yields the potential for unlimited abundance.

_____

_____

_____

ABOUT THE AUTHOR

Sheila Willis
San Diego, California
Certified Abundance Coach/Transformation Speaker/Author
www.lifecoachsheilawillis.com
bit.ly/shopselfhelpproducts
http://bit.ly/abundancecoachsheila
swillis@lifecoachsheilawillis.com

DAY 68 – LIVING ABUNDANTLY WITH A POSITIVE MINDSET

"As it is within, so it is without" - Hermes Trismegistus

It is impossible for a person to live higher than their thought life. The thoughts that one thinks determine the quality of life. The dominate thoughts manifest into the physical reality in some way, some shape, or some form. Therefore, one can't think thoughts of fear and experience faith. In a like manner one can't have thoughts of hatred and experience love. The negative cancels out the positive or vice versa. They both can't exist at the same time. Therefore, choose wisely and embrace a positive mindset to live abundantly.

_____

_____

_____

ABOUT THE AUTHOR

Sheila Willis
San Diego, California
Certified Abundance Coach/Transformation Speaker/Author
www.lifecoachsheilawillis.com
bit.ly/shopselfhelpproducts
http://bit.ly/abundancecoachsheila
swillis@lifecoachsheilawillis.com

DAY 69 — POWER OF POSITIVE SELF-PERCEPTION PART 1

"Perception believed is reality achieved" – Andy August

Perceptive is everything. No one needs to believe in you for you to succeed but, you must believe in yourself. Based on perception one views the world whether that view is true or not. For example, if one believes that life is scarce then scarcity manifests in life. On the other hand, when one believes in abundance the manifestations of abundance is prevalent in one's reality. What you believe you will accomplish. If the dream wasn't first possible in some form, It couldn't exist in your heart. Keep moving in the direction of your dreams.

_____

_____

_____

ABOUT THE AUTHOR

Sheila Willis
San Diego, California
Certified Abundance Coach/Transformation Speaker/Author
www.lifecoachsheilawillis.com
bit.ly/shopselfhelpproducts
http://bit.ly/abundancecoachsheila
swillis@lifecoachsheilawillis.com

DAY 70 – POWER OF POSITIVE SELF-PERCEPTION PART 2

"Mirror, Mirror on the Wall" – The Queen in Snow White

Our lives are direct reflection of the thought life. The life one lives mirrors the internal thoughts. We are creative beings that create through thoughts which produce words, emotions, and actions. By thoughts one's life experience is either being impaired or created. The manifested experiences reveal the truth that's within. Don't just clean off the mirror, live in the light of truth of one's own reflection. Change your thoughts to change your world. It is possible to change any circumstance with the right tools and a willing renewed mind.

_____

_____

_____

ABOUT THE AUTHOR

Sheila Willis
San Diego, California
Certified Abundance Coach/Transformation Speaker/Author
www.lifecoachsheilawillis.com
bit.ly/shopselfhelpproducts
http://bit.ly/abundancecoachsheila
swillis@lifecoachsheilawillis.com

DAY 71 – POWER OF POSITIVE SELF-PERCEPTION PART 3

"The only limit that exist are those within our minds." ~ Sheila Willis

On occasion, we need to remind ourselves just how strong we really are. Like the way David fought Goliath, an eight feet tall warrior, who threatened Israel's army. No soldier wanted to fight him. However, David, a small shepherd accepted the challenge. No one thought David would win. However, David recalled all of his past victories and saw himself undefeated. Because of his self-perception he obtained the victory. Today, rise despite whatever tries to hinder you and declare yourself a winner.

_____

_____

_____

ABOUT THE AUTHOR

Sheila Willis
San Diego, California
Certified Abundance Coach/Transformation Speaker/Author
www.lifecoachsheilawillis.com
bit.ly/shopselfhelpproducts
http://bit.ly/abundancecoachsheila
swillis@lifecoachsheilawillis.com

DAY 72 – MASTER THE MINDSET OF FAITH

"If you want to fly you must give up what holds you down" - Anonymous

Currency in the physical world is money but, the exchange in the nonphysical (spiritual) world is faith. Faith the size of a mustard seed moves mountains. What an awesome conversion rate!

Faith is always in the present tense. It's not believing it shall happen but, knowing that it has already happened. Everything visible was created from that which is invisible. Faith is the evidence that, what you hope for already exists in the non-physical. Practicing faith brings substance from the intangible and invisible, causing it to manifest in the visible world.

_____

_____

_____

ABOUT THE AUTHOR

Sheila Willis
San Diego, California
Certified Abundance Coach/Transformation Speaker/Author
www.lifecoachsheilawillis.com
bit.ly/shopselfhelpproducts
http://bit.ly/abundancecoachsheila
swillis@lifecoachsheilawillis.com

DAY 73 – CREATE LIFE WITH FIERCE FAITH

"Faith and fear are both states of mind, choose wisely" – Sheila Willis

The profound question "What is in your hands?" was asked of Moses by God when he became intimidated by the assignment given to him.

God wanted him to realize that He would use what Moses already possessed. He had to exercise faith to align with his purpose. This tool became a powerful weapon in his hands and brought forth miracles on his behalf and others. So, *what's in your hands?* It is those things you possess that will bring forth victory in every challenge and propel you forward.

_____

_____

_____

ABOUT THE AUTHOR

Sheila Willis
San Diego, California
Certified Abundance Coach/Transformation Speaker/Author
www.lifecoachsheilawillis.com
bit.ly/shopselfhelpproducts
http://bit.ly/abundancecoachsheila
swillis@lifecoachsheilawillis.com

DAY 74 – KEY TO HAVING IT ALL

"Above all else, guard your heart, for it is the of life" Proverbs 4:23

Above anything else, the scriptures urges us to guard the heart, the core of man's existence. The heart is very valuable for out of this place flows (thoughts, emotions, words, and desires) determines the course of one's life. Further, the heart connects God and man and one's passions and dreams. The heart, being the source of everything one does, needs to be healthy. When it is unhealthy, it spills over into other key places in life.

Engage in prayer, meditation, and recreation to keep your heart spiritually healthy.

_____

_____

_____

ABOUT THE AUTHOR

Sheila Willis
San Diego, California
Certified Abundance Coach/Transformation Speaker/Author
www.lifecoachsheilawillis.com
bit.ly/shopselfhelpproducts
http://bit.ly/abundancecoachsheila
swillis@lifecoachsheilawillis.com

DAY 75 — YOU ARE ALREADY AMAZING

"The true beauty of a woman is reflected in her soul." – Audrey Hepburn

There is now an awakening and return to the divine feminine energy. Women are awesome, magnificent, mysterious, magical, amazing, and glorious beings. Yes, you read it right "glorious." Wars have been fought over women and kings have bowed. A man named Jacob (Genesis 28) worked 14 years to obtain the love of a woman he had never touched. Oh, the glorious mystery of feminine energy. When a woman knows her value she is powerful, unstoppable, and unforgettable.

_____

_____

_____

ABOUT THE AUTHOR

Sheila Willis
San Diego, California
Certified Abundance Coach/Transformation Speaker/Author
www.lifecoachsheilawillis.com
bit.ly/shopselfhelpproducts
http://bit.ly/abundancecoachsheila
swillis@lifecoachsheilawillis.com

DAY 76 – OVERCOMING FINANCIAL ILLITERACY

"The real tragedy of the poor is the poverty of their aspirations." - Adam Smith

During a conversation at a financial seminar, I noticed that certain people did not need to be there. And, those that needed to be there were not present. That is how it usually goes, isn't it? The rich continue to educate themselves about finances and the poor generally do not attend wealth building seminars. Their minds need to develop a financial mindset by attending financial seminars, coaching, and reading books. Devour knowledge and become financially literate then you will overcome.

_____

_____

_____

ABOUT THE AUTHOR

Sheila Willis
San Diego, California
Certified Abundance Coach/Transformation Speaker/Author
www.lifecoachsheilawillis.com
bit.ly/shopselfhelpproducts
http://bit.ly/abundancecoachsheila
swillis@lifecoachsheilawillis.com

DAY 77 — PEACE RULES

And let the peace of God rule in your hearts, to which also you were called in one body; and be thankful. Colossians 3:15 (WEB)

Difficulties, struggles, challenges, and mistakes happen. When you allow these circumstances to dictate your happiness, you risk missing out on God's abundant life. It was never his intention for you to live one day on cloud nine and the next day down in the dumps. Uncertainty increases your stress level and creates a sense of insecurity. God wants you to live consistently and enjoy every single day of your life. Let God's peace rule.

_____

_____

_____

ABOUT THE AUTHOR

Jennifer Biggins is from Cordele, Georgia and resides in Ocala, Florida. She is a proud graduate of Lake Region high school. Jennifer is passionate about caring for children, whose families are in the middle of transitions.
DNW21@gmail.com
www.independentlydevelopinganewway.com
www.facebook.com/IDNW21
www.linkedin.com/in/idnw21
twitter.com/idnw21
www.instagram.com/idanw21

DAY 78 – GLORIFY GOD WITH YOUR BODY

"Or do you not know that your body is the temple of the Holy Spirit who is in you." - 1 Corinthians 6: 19

Will you invite a King to a dirty, run down, non-functional house? Of course not! Then, why you don't take care of your body which is the temple of the Holy Spirit and the vessel God use to do His work in earth? All things are lawful, but all things are not beneficial. So, eating nutrient dense foods, practicing self-care, exercising and meditating in the Word of God will keep your body healthy and strong to do God's work.

_____

_____

_____

ABOUT THE AUTHOR

She's a Holistic Health Practitioner and Coach with over 24+ years as a RMA and Lab Tech.
Aida Cirino-Lee RMA AADP CHIC
Website: www.rx4everhealth.com
Email: info@rx4everhealth.com
Facebook: aidacirinolee
Facebook business page: www.facebook.com/rx4everlastinghealth
Instagram: @rx4everhealth
Twitter: rx4everhealth

DAY 79 – THE POWER OF YOUR TONGUE

"Life and death are in the power of the tongue." - Proverbs 18: 21(part a)

The power of life and death, lack and prosperity and even health and sickness are in your tongue. Your tongue is the smallest organ, but it can corrupt the whole body. When you speak, you can choose to curse or bless. So, speak words that bring life, freedom and inspiration to yourself and to others. Use affirmations to speak life, light and prosperity in to your life to boost your, faith, confidence and your health.

_____

_____

_____

ABOUT THE AUTHOR

She's a Holistic Health Practitioner and Coach with over 24+ years as a RMA and Lab Tech.
Aida Cirino-Lee RMA AADP CHIC
Website: www.rx4everhealth.com
Email: info@rx4everhealth.com
Facebook: aidacirinolee
Facebook business page: www.facebook.com/rx4everlastinghealth
Instagram: @rx4everhealth
Twitter: rx4everhealth

DAY 80 – MONEY MATTERS PART 1

"Money is the answer for all things."- Ecclesiastes 10:19

Money is simply a tool. Money is neither good nor evil, it is neutral. The person possessing money determines its uses. People who struggle with money generally have negative thoughts about it. Some may think it is wrong to have an abundance of money thinking, that it is evil or greedy. The truth is, it is impossible live beyond your thoughts. Without a change, many live in a state of scarcity.

_____

_____

_____

ABOUT THE AUTHOR

Sheila Willis
San Diego, California
Certified Abundance Coach/Transformation Speaker/Author
www.lifecoachsheilawillis.com
bit.ly/shopselfhelpproducts
http://bit.ly/abundancecoachsheila
swillis@lifecoachsheilawillis.com

DAY 81 – MONEY MATTERS PART 2

"Money is the answer for all things."- Ecclesiastes 10:19

Examine your belief about money. Ask if these beliefs hinder or assist in attracting money. Be willing to let go of any belief that do not serve or establish the attraction of money. Make necessary adjustments in your thoughts about money. How can you attract something that your thoughts repel? To attract money, you need to feel good about it. Begin thinking about all the good money can bring to you and your family.

_____

_____

_____

ABOUT THE AUTHOR

Sheila Willis
San Diego, California
Certified Abundance Coach/Transformation Speaker/Author
www.lifecoachsheilawillis.com
bit.ly/shopselfhelpproducts
http://bit.ly/abundancecoachsheila
swillis@lifecoachsheilawillis.com

DAY 82 – CREATING MORE ABUNDANCE

"Abundance is not something we acquire. It is something we tune into." - Wayne Dyer

Words are manifestation of the thought life. Don't share from a scarcity mindset. Your language should speak only of prosperity and abundance. Don't say things like, "I can't afford that" or, "I don't have enough money." Immediately correct negative self-talk by stating a positive affirmation. For example, instead of saying, "I don't have enough money," say something like, "I believe in an abundant universe, therefore money is on its way to me."

_____

_____

_____

ABOUT THE AUTHOR

Sheila Willis
San Diego, California
Certified Abundance Coach/Transformation Speaker/Author
www.lifecoachsheilawillis.com
bit.ly/shopselfhelpproducts
http://bit.ly/abundancecoachsheila
swillis@lifecoachsheilawillis.com

DAY 83 – FIRST STEP TO MONEY CREATION

"Successful People Make Money" - Wayne Dyer

Sowing and Reaping a universal law determines how money comes into your life. This law operates by the actions and feelings that your life expresses as seeds are sown. Thus, the conditions that come in life are the harvest reaped. Therefore, to try and obtain things without giving or sowing violates this law whether its dealing with finances or in other areas. And, in turn the actions are unfruitful. When you sow, expect to reap.

_____

_____

_____

ABOUT THE AUTHOR

Sheila Willis
San Diego, California
Certified Abundance Coach/Transformation Speaker/Author
www.lifecoachsheilawillis.com
bit.ly/shopselfhelpproducts
http://bit.ly/abundancecoachsheila
swillis@lifecoachsheilawillis.com

DAY 84 – MASTER THE MINDSET OF WEALTH

"For God did not give us a spirit of timidity (of cowardice, of craven and cringing and fawning fear), but [He has given us a spirit] of power and of love and of calm and well-balanced mind and discipline and self-control." - 2 Timothy 1:7 AMPC

When it comes to money, many millennials fear dealing with their money problems and may pray for someone else to take care of it. But with guidance, they can face their fears now and make steps to overcome them. You can take those fears and become fearless warriors by taking on those challenges to start building wealth. How can I help you build your wealth?

_____

_____

_____

ABOUT THE AUTHOR

I am a Money Coach who coaches millennials to find their lost money and build their wealth.
Chantel Tavares
Orlando, FL
Email: Tavaresconsulting.fl@gmail.com
Website: Tavaresfba.com
Facebook: https://www.facebook.com/tavaresconsulting.fl/
Instagram: https://www.instagram.com/tavareschantel/
LinkedIn: https://www.linkedin.com/in/chanteltavares/

DAY 85 – PATIENCE IS THE KEY TO WEALTH

"Trust (lean on, reply on, and be confident) in the Lord and do good; so shall you dwell in the land and feed surely on his faithfulness, and truly you shall be fed."
- Psalm 37:3 AMPC

When it comes to growing your money, patience is the key. Whether patience in saving money to move to a better neighborhood or to start your business. Without it, you can end up hurting yourself and slowing the process to your success. You can practice patience and build habits to help you reach your money and life goals. How can I help you build your patience to your wealth?

_____

_____

_____

ABOUT THE AUTHOR

I am a Money Coach who coaches millennials to find their lost money and build their wealth.
Chantel Tavares
Orlando, FL
Email: Tavaresconsulting.fl@gmail.com
Website: Tavaresfba.com
Facebook: https://www.facebook.com/tavaresconsulting.fl/
Instagram: https://www.instagram.com/tavareschantel/
LinkedIn: https://www.linkedin.com/in/chanteltavares/

DAY 86 — SEEK GOD FIRST

"But seek ye first the kingdom of God, and his righteousness; and all these things shall be added unto you."- Matthew 6:33 (KJV)

Money is certainly one measure of gain. It is one of many; enjoy living in prosperity "according to His riches in glory!" Money is simply a tool that can be used for God's glory. The true riches are in seeking and achieving His best for you. Sometimes, that includes money. Many times, it includes blessings far greater than money. The true riches are in His glory! "Seek and ye shall find."

_____

_____

_____

ABOUT THE AUTHOR

Rachel Leigh, MBA/ Author/ Speaker/ Coach
Jackson, Tennessee
RachelLeigh0180@gmail.com
Facebook page: Living Water Bible Studies
www.facebook.com/WarriorAngelMinistries

DAY 87 — WAITING ON GOD

"But those who wait on the Lord shall renew their strength; They shall mount up with wings like eagles, They shall run and not be weary, They shall walk and not faint." - Isaiah 40:31

Waiting definitely isn't something many of us like to do. However, waiting on God is worth the wait. In waiting on the Lord, it gives us a chance to realize that we are not God. Stepping back and letting him be in control, lets God work internally on us. Many times, we pray for things not realizing God has to prepare us for them. Waiting on the Lord strengthens our faith. It is He who makes us whole and gives us what no man can.

ABOUT THE AUTHOR

Dominicia Hill is a network marketing professional with a passion for educating others on financial literacy while getting their financial affairs in order.
queenfaithbey@gmail.com
Facebook Www.facebook.com/Queenfaith19
IG www.instagram.com/QUEENFAITH_Consultant.Mentor

DAY 88 – DREAM BECAME A REALITY

"But Jesus looked at them and said, "With man this is impossible, but with God all things are possible." - Matthew 19: 26

Here's my testimony of faith. One day I was working and the next day I was unemployed. I signed a contract to purchase a home and the closing was October 22nd. On September 13th, I was laid off. The bank called my job to reconfirm employment and the secretary was away from her desk, thus the president answered the phone. The president said "Yes, she's employed," and here I am 25 years later in the same home! God is so faithful and He will work in your favor!

_____

_____

_____

ABOUT THE AUTHOR

Patricia Scott is a retired special education teacher, with a desire to motivate students to believe in their dreams.
Patricia Scott
Chesapeake, Virginia
pscott675@gmail.com
https://www.facebook.com/kyrkwacyrmarq1990

DAY 89 – LIVE YOUR BEST LIFE

"Always live your life like it's golden by being authentic." - Tina M. Fernandez

LIVE YOUR BEST LIFE AS ONLY YOU CAN DEFINE! Live YOUR best life as only you can! In order to do this, you have to create your balance, restore your rhythm, love unconditionally, give of yourself unselfishly and forgive often. Your definition of you is crafted only by your authentic self. Know who you are, whose you are and hold on to your truths without compromise. Cherish each day by making a difference both inside and outside of the home. Then you will live YOUR best life as only you can!

_____

_____

_____

ABOUT THE AUTHOR

Founder of the Inspired Leadership Institute, where we equip, empower and inspire the 21st-century leader.
Tina M. Fernandez, MBA
Inspiresolutionsgroup@gmail.com
https://tmfernandez35.wixsite.com/inspiredleaders

DAY 90 – STEP FORWARD, STEP QUICKLY, STEP WITH A PURPOSE AND SHINE!

"Always live your life like it's golden by being authentic." - Tina M. Fernandez

Isn't it time for you to take a step forward, to do it quickly and with a purpose? You know what you need to do and how to do it. You understand the purpose of taking this step and you know it is the right thing to do. Take a deep breath step forward with confidence! Move quickly with purpose. Know that God has given you this special gift and it's your time to SHINE.

_____

_____

_____

ABOUT THE AUTHOR

Founder of the Inspired Leadership Institute, where we equip, empower and inspire the 21st-century leader.
Tina M. Fernandez, MBA
Inspiresolutionsgroup@gmail.com
https://tmfernandez35.wixsite.com/inspiredleaders

DAY 91 – FAITH PART 1

"And we walk by FAITH, not by sight." - 2 Corinthians 5:7

Looking back, I reflect on my childhood. I was raised in a single parent household, with a mother and grandmother so strong that the absence of a father figure wasn't even missed. They were prayer warriors. It didn't have to be Sunday in church or religious functions...they would just break out in prayer no matter where. They both had the faith of Job! No problem too big, because they had something bigger.... FAITH!!!

_____

_____

_____

ABOUT THE AUTHOR

Dr. Charlette Fairchild (Charlie) is a 1981 graduate of ODU and went on to receive her Masters and Doctorate from The College of William and Mary.
Dr. Charlie Fairchild
Suffolk, Virginia
Facebook - Charlie Fairchild
Linked In & IG - Dr. Charlette Fairchild
Twitter - Charlie@DrCharlette

DAY 92 — FAITH PART 2

"And we walk by FAITH, not by sight." - 2 Corinthians 5:7

Faith is:

- growing up poor, but believing you had it all!
- watching someone ill and knowing everything is going to be alright.
- being hungry, but knowing another meal is coming. being homeless, but knowing shelter will be provided.
- seeing your vision and realizing one day you will achieve it.

Faith is the substance of things hoped for and the evidence of things not seen! Have faith. Tomorrow is going to be great!

_____

_____

_____

ABOUT THE AUTHOR

Dr. Charlette Fairchild (Charlie) is a 1981 graduate of ODU and went on to receive her Masters and Doctorate from The College of William and Mary.
Dr. Charlie Fairchild
Suffolk, Virginia
Facebook - Charlie Fairchild
Linked In & IG - Dr. Charlette Fairchild
Twitter - Charlie@DrCharlette

DAY 93 – JUST DO IT – STAY LASER FOCUSED (PART I)

"Commit to the Lord whatever you do, and he will establish your plans." - Proverbs 16:3 (NIV)

Remain focused on the outcome of everything you do in every day and in every way. You will be encouraged and inspired to keep going. Figure out what is important to you, what your values are, and make a plan to get there – and you will succeed. Do not let anyone else determine your success. Remember, a high-paying corporate job does not necessarily mean satisfaction or fulfillment.

_____

_____

_____

ABOUT THE AUTHOR

Velma is a retired executive, author, and speaker. Velma has written two books, "Too Many, Too Soon" and "A Look Back."
Velma Jackson-Wilkins
www.velmajacksonwilkins.com
velmajacksonwilkins@gmail.com
www.facebook.com/velma-jackson-wilkins

DAY 94 – STAY LASER FOCUSED (PART 2)

"But as for you, be strong and do not give up, for your work will be rewarded." - Chronicles 15:7 (NIV)

Count your blessings and be happy if you have a good position that you enjoy especially if it leads you to a place you desire. Be decisive and determined and don't give up until you see the light. Don't let detours, exits, and speed bumps in the road prevent you from achieving your professional goals.

Keep your eyes steadfast on the prize – only you, with the Lord's guidance, can determine what that prize is.

_____

_____

_____

ABOUT THE AUTHOR

Velma is a retired executive, author, and speaker. Velma has written two books, "Too Many, Too Soon" and "A Look Back."
www.velmajacksonwilkins.com
velmajacksonwilkins@gmail.com
www.facebook.com/velma-jackson-wilkins

DAY 95 – DO NOT LET YOUR DIAGNOSIS AFFECT YOUR FAITH

"I shall not die, but live, and declare the works of the LORD." - Psalm 118:17 (KJV)

At the age of three, my mother taught me about fasting and praying. These two tools provided me with the instruments that would sustain my very life at the age of thirty-five. I went to the doctor and my diagnosis was HIV. I was not moved by diagnosis, but I fasted and prayed. My end results were: negative and victory! God came and healed me from HIV! I shall live!

_____

_____

_____

ABOUT THE AUTHOR

Look for Healing in the Vessel Mother's Love, A Daughter's Journey of Faith book on www.healinginthevesselministries.com.
Jacqueline Goodwin
Hopkins South Carolina
www.healinginthevesselministries.com
www.facebook.com/lenisegoodwin
instagram:lenisegoodwin

DAY 96 – WAITING ON GOD WILL TEST YOUR FAITH

"Wait on the LORD: be of good courage, and he shall strengthen thine heart: wait, I say, on the LORD." – Psalm 27:14 (KJV)

Waiting on God is like baking a cake. After stirring all the ingredients in a bowl, we must place it in the oven and wait until it is done. Our trials are the oven and we want to come out of the trial too early. Just wait. I lost my house to foreclosure and now I am renting. However, I am rising like the cake above the heat with faith!

_____

_____

_____

ABOUT THE AUTHOR

Look for Healing in the Vessel Mother's Love, A Daughter's Journey of Faith book on www.healinginthevesselministries.com.
Jacqueline Goodwin
Hopkins South Carolina
www.healinginthevesselministries.com
www.facebook.com/lenisegoodwin
instagram:lenisegoodwin

DAY 97 – OVERCOMING ANXIETY

"Which of you by worrying can add one cubit to his stature?" - Matthew 6:27 (NKJV)

Anxiety is real. Symptoms can vary from mild uneasiness to a pervasive worry that results in very real feelings of panic, fear and nervousness. As a mental health professional and from a personal perspective I can say, there is hope. I suggest finding a licensed mental health clinician in your area or online. Depending upon the root of the anxiety a combination of prayer, therapy, and even medication, when needed can help reduce the symptoms.

_____

_____

_____

ABOUT THE AUTHOR

Julie Clockston LCSW Doctoral Candidate has been working in mental health care for 23 years. She specializes in working with individuals who have experienced trauma that allows her to provide special care to individuals who have been victimized.
Julie Clockston, LCSW
Doctor of Social Work Candidate
Denver, Colorado
http://juliejmsw.wixsite.com/counseling
JulieJMSW@gmail.com
https://www.facebook.com/julieclockstoncounseling/

DAY 98 — STOP BELIEVING THE LIES

"And know this: in the last days, times will be hard. [2] You see, the world will be filled with narcissistic, money-grubbing, pretentious, arrogant, and abusive people. They will rebel against their parents and will be ungrateful, unholy, [3] uncaring, coldhearted, accusing, without restraint, savage, and haters of anything good. [4] *Expect them to be* treacherous, reckless, swollen with self-importance, and given to loving pleasure more than they love God. - 2 Timothy 3:1-5 (Voice, 2012).

In my work with survivors of psychological and emotional abuse, I see a lot of wounded souls — individuals who abuse others based on partial truths and full lies. Often victims are targeted and blindsided before they even realize they are being abused. I challenge you to use your intuition. Observe long term actions. It is ok to take precautions and protective measures for yourself and those in your care.

_____

_____

_____

ABOUT THE AUTHOR

Julie Clockston, LCSW
Denver, Colorado
http://juliejmsw.wixsite.com/counseling
JulieJMSW@gmail.com
https://www.facebook.com/julieclockstoncounseling/

DAY 99 – A FAITH LIKE JOB

"Though he slay me, yet will I trust in him..." - Job 13:15 (KJV)

True faith is being able to trust God even in difficult situations. When it feels scary, uncertain or weird, we must still trust God using Gait, Grit and Grace.

Gait: To move forward freely in our faith and finances we must step out even when the path ahead appears turbulent or blurred.

Grit: Our faith in God must hold fast amidst negativity, sickness, rejection or loss.

Grace: We must remember that God's grace is enough.

_____

_____

_____

ABOUT THE AUTHOR

Victoria Melhado-Daley
Health Care Professional for over 10 years, Author, Serial Entrepreneur [Success & Wellness Coach, International Speaker, Certified Travel Specialist and Globe Trotter]
Facebook Page: Victoria Melhado Daley
https://www.facebook.com/EscapetoParadiseWithVictoria
VicMelhadoDaley@Twitter
victoriamelhadodaley@Instagram
www.victoriamelhadodaley.org

DAY 100 – THROUGH EYES OF FAITH

"Now faith is the substance of things hoped for, the evidence of things not seen."
- Hebrews 11:1 (KJV)

Faith takes us on a 3D journey where we manifest the blueprint long before the building is completed. Through faith we can ascend the steps of adversity into the surreal streets of gold and a land that overflows with milk and honey. Faith makes unpleasant experiences more tolerable. Faith is the tangible foundation that gives the believer hope during tribulation, fear, or pain. The pillars of Hope reinforce Faith. Faith is perpetual knowledge, understanding and confidence in God's supremacy. Faith supersedes sight.

_____

_____

_____

ABOUT THE AUTHOR

Victoria Melhado-Daley
Health Care Professional for over 10 years, Author, Serial Entrepreneur [Success & Wellness Coach, International Speaker, Certified Travel Specialist and Globe Trotter]
Facebook Page: Victoria Melhado Daley
https://www.facebook.com/EscapetoParadiseWithVictoria
VicMelhadoDaley@Twitter
victoriamelhadodaley@Instagram
www.victoriamelhadodaley.org

DAY 101 – POWER TO CREATE WEALTH

"But thou shalt remember the Lord thy God: for it is he that giveth thee power to get wealth" - Deuteronomy 8:18 (KJV)

It is so exciting to know that God wants us to be blessed! However, being wealthy does not only mean having increased finances or material possessions. God wants his people to enjoy a life of abundance that overflows with good health, peace of mind, and financial satisfaction.

God's word reminds us that he gives us the creative ability to discover, produce, generate and multiply wealth in our lives. We can live bountifully everyday knowing we are blessed and knowing also that we have the power to be a blessing.

_____

_____

_____

ABOUT THE AUTHOR

Victoria Melhado-Daley
Health Care Professional for over 10 years, Author, Serial Entrepreneur [Success & Wellness Coach, International Speaker, Certified Travel Specialist and Globe Trotter]
Facebook Page: Victoria Melhado Daley
https://www.facebook.com/EscapetoParadiseWithVictoria
VicMelhadoDaley@Twitter
victoriamelhadodaley@Instagram
www.victoriamelhadodaley.org

DAY 102 – FREE INDEED!

"The thief cometh not, but for to steal, and to kill, and to destroy: I am come that they might have life, and that they might have it more abundantly." - John 10:10 (KJV)

Isn't it liberating to know that you have been exonerated? Well, you should be absolutely elated and off your rockers! Just imagine being found guilty for committing a crime. Then, a very wealthy stranger comes along, pays the bail and hires a successful attorney for you! That's it! Suddenly, the jail cell opens; you are given a robe and cash and are told to walk free! That is the love, mercy and grace of God towards us. God does not only give us spiritual and physical freedom, but also allows us to live a rich and satisfying life. God is Jehovah Nissi – Our Banner and he makes us abundantly free.

_____

_____

_____

ABOUT THE AUTHOR

Victoria Melhado-Daley
Health Care Professional for over 10 years, Author, Serial Entrepreneur [Success & Wellness Coach, International Speaker, Certified Travel Specialist and Globe Trotter]
Facebook Page: Victoria Melhado Daley
https://www.facebook.com/EscapetoParadiseWithVictoria
VicMelhadoDaley@Twitter
victoriamelhadodaley@Instagram
www.victoriamelhadodaley.org

DAY 103 – THE SOURCE OF WEALTH IS HAPPINESS, PROSPERITY AND ABUNDANCE : PART 1

"For I know the plans I have for you," declares the LORD, "plans to prosper you and not to harm you, plans to give you hope and a future." - Jeremiah 29:11

Believers miss out on blessings when they embrace the idea that their time on earth is dedicated to sojourning, laboring, and enduring life only in hopes that one day we will be rewarded.

Prosperity is your birthright, but it takes applied knowledge and wisdom for a good man or women to leave an inheritance to their family.

Strategically, learn the rules of wealth and experience financial freedom.

_____

_____

_____

ABOUT THE AUTHOR

Kimberly Mcfarlane is a Certified Financial Educator, Mompreneur offering wealth creation strategies.
www.kimberlymcfarlane.com
results@kimberlymcfarlane.com
www.newmoneysources.com
https://bit.ly/Linkedin_KMcfarlane
https://www.facebook.com/KimberlyMoneyMentor/

DAY 104 – THE SOURCE OF WEALTH IS HAPPINESS, PROSPERITY AND ABUNDANCE : PART 2

"By wisdom, a house is built, and through understanding, it is established; through knowledge, its rooms are filled with rare and beautiful treasures." - (Proverbs 24:3-4)

The entire world was created through words and wisdom. Our words create our reality. Without realizing it, we speak death over our lives when we think of lack, speak of limitation or believe there is a shortage of what we desire to manifest.

As children of God, let us take control of our words and command prosperity into our lives. God created us to have dominion, to prosper and to rule.

ABOUT THE AUTHOR

Kimberly Mcfarlane is a Certified Financial Educator, Mompreneur offering wealth creation strategies.
www.kimberlymcfarlane.com
results@kimberlymcfarlane.com
www.newmoneysources.com
https://bit.ly/Linkedin_KMcfarlane
https://www.facebook.com/KimberlyMoneyMentor/

DAY 105 – WHO SAID YOU CAN'T DO IT?

[13] I can do all things through Christ which strengtheneth me. – Phil 4:13

As a Latina, I have often dealt with many challenges personally as well as professionally. Coming from a country where the male was given certain privileges in the household always pushed me to be different. Going against the norm in my family was quite the challenge. After they told me I couldn't do this or that, I would work harder at it. I am the first female in my family who will have a doctorate degree by 2019! Not only did I accomplish this, I have seven practicing licenses, my own clinic and a few blogs. Who said you can't do it? Believe in yourself always!

_____

_____

_____

ABOUT THE AUTHOR

Dr. Soraya Sawicki is the founder of Infinity Integrated Counseling and Spa Services, LLC. Soraya practices psychotherapy and is an expert on relationship issues and vicarious trauma.
Dr. Soraya Sawicki, MSW, LCSW
Doctor of Social Work
Farmington, Connecticut
Sorayasawicki@aol.com
http://infinity-integrated.com/

DAY 106 – DO YOU PRACTICE SELF-CARE?

"If I am not for myself, who will be for me" - Elder Hillel

Self-care has been deemed the number one factor in positive performance, improving overall wellness, and healthy living. However, studies show that individuals fail to engage in their personal self-care. Many healthcare professionals surprisingly do not practice self-care, in addition, recent studies also show that other professionals also fail to practice self-care leaving them at risk. In the long run lack of self-care, may result in physical or psychological distress. If you are in the helping profession or a caregiver, ask yourself, "am I taking care of myself, because if I don't, who will?"

_____

_____

_____

ABOUT THE AUTHOR

Dr. Soraya Sawicki is the founder of Infinity Integrated Counseling and Spa Services, LLC. Soraya practices psychotherapy and is an expert on relationship issues and vicarious trauma.
Dr. Soraya Sawicki, MSW, LCSW
Doctor of Social Work
Farmington, Connecticut
Sorayasawicki@aol.com
http://infinity-integrated.com/

DAY 107 – PREPARE FOR IMPACT

"Where no counsel is, the people fall: but in the multitude of counsellors there is safety." - Proverbs 11:14 (KJV)

Think about being on an airplane. Wrap your mind around the words, "Flight attendants prepare for landing." Now consider these words, "Flight attendants prepare for impact." Preparing for landing and preparing for impact yield very different feelings. A landing is easy and comfortable and relatively safe. Impact brings fear and distress. It can be dangerous, even deadly. But with impact there is also opportunity, innovation and possibility. Prepare for impact because the reward is greater than just a landing!

_____

_____

_____

ABOUT THE AUTHOR

Marla Godette has earned degrees in Early Childhood Education, Human Services, and Counseling. Currently she is pursuing a doctorate degree in Global Leadership.
Marla Godette
mentoringmomentsllc@gmail.com
Facebook - Mentoring Moments LLC and Marla L Godette
Twitter - @thewifeinlaw1| Instagram - @mlgodette

DAY 108 – WORRY VERSUS CONCERN

"Where no counsel is, the people fall: but in the multitude of counsellors there is safety." - Proverbs 11:14 (KJV)

Worry will invade our mental space causing emotional distress and physical anguish. When we worry, we do nothing but worry. Concern however, calls for action. When we become concerned we do things. We make phone calls to check on a missed friend. We do extra work to reach our professional goals. So, the next time you are paralyzed with worry, get up and take action! Let concern run the show.

_____

_____

_____

ABOUT THE AUTHOR

Marla Godette has earned degrees in Early Childhood Education, Human Services, and Counseling. Currently she is pursuing a doctorate degree in Global Leadership.
Marla Godette
mentoringmomentsllc@gmail.com
Facebook - Mentoring Moments LLC and Marla L Godette
Twitter - @thewifeinlaw1| Instagram - @mlgodette

DAY 109 – MOVING FROM NOT ENOUGH INTO MORE THAN ENOUGH WHILE MAKING THE SAME PAY

"Steady plodding brings prosperity; hasty speculation brings poverty." - Proverbs 21:5

Society and our families have taught us how to manage our bills by telling us, go to school, get a good job, and pay our bills. What they did not teach us is how to manage our money.

This inspired me to become a Money Coach, I accomplish this by teaching a simple four step process on how to manage your money. This leads to closing the gap to financial freedom and creating generational wealth within our families.

_____

_____

_____

ABOUT THE AUTHOR

Susan Jones
Deltona, Florida
www.facebook.com/Without A Doubt Finance Education and Services

DAY 110 – AN ATTITUDE OF GRATITUDE

"Give thanks to the Lord , for he is good! His faithful love endures forever." -
Psalm 107:1

A great tool to remind you of God's faithfulness is to keep a blessing journal. Take time each day to write in your journal a short list of four to five of your blessings. As you do this daily, you will see your perspective on life begin to shift.

_____

_____

_____

ABOUT THE AUTHOR

Shawnee Penkacik is a wife to her husband Jason of twenty-two years, a mom to eleven amazing children ranging in age from 4 years to 21, an author, a social media manager, and podcast host. She has found throughout life that God is faithful and celebrates daily that the joy of the Lord is her strength. She loves to encourage and remind moms that they are enough in Christ.
www.sunshinythoughts.com
https://www.facebook.com/shawneepenkacik/

DAY 111 – GOD WANTS YOU TO PROSPER

"God takes pleasure in the prosperity of His servants." - Psalm 35:27

Finances are the foundation of life and your quality of life. Women need to know how important it is to know the topic of finance and how to properly position ourselves with it. This will lead us on a path to prosper mentally, emotionally, spiritually, and financially.

_____

_____

_____

ABOUT THE AUTHOR

Janet "Michelle" Wood
Montgomery, Alabama

DAY 112 – TRIALS TO TREASURE

"And for we know that in all things God works for good of those who love him, who have been called according to his purpose." - Romans 8:28

Many of us have been through trials both good and bad. These trials make us stronger. These same trials can help us help others. For example, I have taken trials of losing children, having special needs children, even domestic violence and turned it around to help others. I have learned that we can help others through good causes, nonprofits, our churches and neighborhoods. And, we can also monetize our lived experiences through the world of business and more.

ABOUT THE AUTHOR

Teresa Wright Johnson
Atlanta, Georgia
Parent Educator, Speaker, Trainer, Coach, Author
www.twjme.com
https://www.facebook.com/mommycarebiz

DAY 113 — TODAY IS A GIFT

"It takes as much energy to wish as it does to plan." Eleanor Roosevelt.

Freedom – a simple word, that means "the power or right to act, speak, or think as one wants without hindrance or restraint." We should live our lives like there is no tomorrow, enjoying each day and appreciating those around us. Take a moment to stop and smell a flower and enjoy a conversation with a stranger. Live today in such a way to have no regrets.

_____

_____

_____

ABOUT THE AUTHOR

Melanie Campbell
Central Florida
www.hire-it-out.com
melanie@hire-it-out.com
https://www.facebook.com/melaniehireitout
linkedin.com/in/melaniecampbell3

DAY 114 – REAL STRUGGLE

"In that day their burden will be lifted from their shoulders; their yoke from your neck; the yoke will be broken because you have grown so fat." - Isiah 10:27 (NIV)

Burden. Challenge. Struggle. These words have similar meaning yet are different, depending on the circumstance. Big Mama always told me, "Just keep on living, one day you will experience real struggle."

Burdens, challenges, and struggles fade away. When they do, share your testimony. We never know who we can influence or encourage through our life experiences. Be a beacon for change. My personal motto is, "Lift as you climb." What's yours?

_____

_____

_____

ABOUT THE AUTHOR

Dr. Stephanie G. Adams is an Educator, Trainer, Presenter, and the President of a non-profit organization, Voice of Diversity.
Stephanie G. Adams, Ed.D
Fayetteville, Arkansas
www.voiceofdiversity.org
stephgadams@gmail.com
Instagram:@sgadams91

DAY 115 – LOVE UNCONDITIONALLY

"Beloved, let us love one another: for love is God; and every one that loveth is begotten of God, and knoweth God." - I John 4:7 (NIV)

When resolving to make life changes, rarely do we commit to love one another. Love is natural when given to family and close friends. The challenge to love comes when someone does you harm.

God expects you to unconditionally love one other, despite any and all harm imposed upon you. This is not easy, but, as Christians, it is expected. Commit daily to love one another as God loves you.

_____

_____

_____

ABOUT THE AUTHOR

Dr. Stephanie G. Adams is an Educator, Trainer, Presenter, and the President of a non-profit organization, Voice of Diversity.
Stephanie G. Adams, Ed.D
Fayetteville, Arkansas
www.voiceofdiversity.org
stephgadams@gmail.com
Instagram:@sgadams91

DAY 116 – EDUCATION TRUTHS

"The heart of the discerning acquires knowledge, for the ears of the wise seek it out." Proverbs 18:15 (NIV)

I have always thought education was important. This was instilled in me at a very young age. Neither my grandmother or mother attended college, but both women told me I would. Growing up in a low socioeconomic environment, sacrifices were made, and challenges had to be superseded.

All levels of education are obtainable with a supportive network, internal fortitude, drive, and determination. Be encouraged and don't let anyone tell you otherwise.

_____

_____

_____

ABOUT THE AUTHOR

Dr. Stephanie G. Adams is an Educator, Trainer, Presenter, and the President of a non-profit organization, Voice of Diversity.
Stephanie G. Adams, Ed.D
Fayetteville, Arkansas
www.voiceofdiversity.org
stephgadams@gmail.com
Instagram:@sgadams91

DAY 117 – MONEY HARDSHIPS

"The plans of the diligent lead to profit as surely as haste leads to poverty".
Proverbs 21:5 (NIV)

How much do we depend on money? Some say, "Money makes the world go around." Money is a source of survival for without it, we could not pay for the things we need and want.

Unfortunately, money is not received consistently or equally so it is difficult to budget, save, and invest when you must focus on food, shelter, and health.

Manage wisely, seek counseling when needed and stay prayerful.

_____

_____

_____

ABOUT THE AUTHOR

Dr. Stephanie G. Adams is an Educator, Trainer, Presenter, and the President of a non-profit organization, Voice of Diversity.
Stephanie G. Adams, Ed.D
Fayetteville, Arkansas
www.voiceofdiversity.org
stephgadams@gmail.com
Instagram:@sgadams91

DAY 118 – FREEDEMPTION

> "The Spirit of the Lord God is upon me; because the Lord has anointed me to preach good tidings to the poor; he has sent me to heal the brokenhearted, to proclaim liberty to the captives, and the opening of the prison to those who are bound." - Isaiah 61:1 (NKJV)

The prophet Isaiah was on a mission to deliver good news from God. Where we were once captive to sin, we have now been redeemed through God's grace. Unfortunately, we have become so accustomed to living a life full of guilt from our past, that we can't enjoy the freedom in the grace we have received. List five situations over the past year where you received God's grace. Look at how God has been gracious toward you.

_____

_____

_____

ABOUT THE AUTHOR

Dr. Nayshon T. Mosley ("Dr. Nay") is a mother, educator, author, speaker, mentor and advocate from the south side of Chicago, Illinois.
https://gumroad.com/drnayshon
drntmosley@gmail.com @drnayshon (Twitter)
@doctornay (IG)

DAY 119 – REMAINING FAITHFUL & FULL OF FAITH

"Then the Lord answered me and said, 'Write the vision and make it plain on tablets, that he may run who reads it.'" - Habakkuk 2:2 (NKJV)

"Write the vision," is God's response to a series of questions from Habakkuk. How many times have we questioned God with who, what, when, where, why, and how?

God doesn't expect us to have all the answers. Our job: remain faithful and full of faith. Jeremiah 29:11 reminds us that His thoughts toward us are positive with an expected outcome. Write your vision and remain faithful, trusting God for His expected outcome.

_____

_____

_____

ABOUT THE AUTHOR

Dr. Nayshon T. Mosley ("Dr. Nay") is a mother, educator, author, speaker, mentor and advocate from the south side of Chicago, Illinois.
https://gumroad.com/drnayshon
drntmosley@gmail.com @drnayshon (Twitter)
@doctornay (IG)

DAY 120 – TRUST GOD - PART 1

"Trust in the Lord with all thine heart; and lean not unto thine own understanding. In all thy ways acknowledge him, and he shall direct thy paths." - Proverbs 3:5-6

Sometimes life will knock you down to a point where you feel like giving up. However, giving up does not present answers to the situation. We, as strong Christian women, have to realize God has equipped us with an anointing that will destroy any yoke or bondage in our lives. From morning until we go to bed at night, we have to meditate and lean on God's word for truth and understanding.

_____

_____

_____

ABOUT THE AUTHOR

As a John Maxwell Coach, Trainer and Speaker, Dr. Michelle Nelson can offer you workshops, and keynote speaking, aiding your personal and professional growth.
https://www.johncmaxwellgroup.com/michellenelson
https://www.linkedin.com/in/dr-michelle-nelson-261bb255
dealstraight@outlook.com

DAY 121 — TRUST GOD - PART 2

"Trust in the Lord with all thine heart; and lean not unto thine own understanding. In all thy ways acknowledge him, and he shall direct thy paths." - Proverbs 3:5-6

Trust God in every situation, knowing He will provide our every need. We must keep the faith and live with expectation. God will bestow blessings, great opportunities, extraordinary favor and victory upon us that might not happen for the next person, because we have extraordinary favor. Fix your eyes on God's grace, and your problems will be turned around, obstacles will be removed, and healing will manifest itself, in Jesus Name.

_____

_____

_____

ABOUT THE AUTHOR

As a John Maxwell Coach, Trainer and Speaker, Dr. Michelle Nelson can offer you workshops, and keynote speaking, aiding your personal and professional growth.
https://www.johncmaxwellgroup.com/michellenelson
https://www.linkedin.com/in/dr-michelle-nelson-261bb255
dealstraight@outlook.com

DAY 122 – YOU WERE NOT MEANT TO BREAK PART 1

"From the end of the earth, I will call to you. When my heart is Overwhelmed, lead me to the rock that is higher than I" - Psalm 6:1

At the Garden of Eden, God proclaimed enmity between Satan and the women, therefore don't be surprised by his attacks. His job is to prevent you from fulfilling your purpose by any means. Hence, this is why he sends storms to your family, doubt for your peace of mind, and questions for the true essence of whom God predestined you to be. He will strategically place stumbling blocks in your path to bring distractions. Set up a prayer closet to pray for specific attacks from the enemy.

_____

_____

_____

ABOUT THE AUTHOR

God's Child. Entrepreneur. President of Kingdom Chamber of Commerce-Orlando.
Author and License Realtor
Claudette A. Robinson
Orlando, Florida
Contact: www. Kingdomchamberc.com
Email: kingdomchamber@gmail.com
www.facebook.com/Orlandochamber

DAY 123 – YOU WERE NOT MEANT TO BREAK PART 2

"From the end of the earth, I will call to you. When my heart is Overwhelmed, lead me to the rock that is higher than I" - Psalm 6:1

The enemy brings despair to get you to feel powerless to the point of giving up. When you're overwhelmed, and you see no way out, remember, you were not made to break. Crawl your way up onto the rock that is higher than you. Reach into the warrior spirit within and just roar! Your strength will emerge, you will realize no devil in hell can stop what is eminent: your destiny!

_____

_____

_____

ABOUT THE AUTHOR

God's Child. Entrepreneur. President of Kingdom Chamber of Commerce-Orlando. Author and License Realtor
Claudette A. Robinson
Orlando, Florida
Contact: www. Kingdomchamberc.com
Email: kingdomchamber@gmail.com
www.facebook.com/Orlandochamber

DAY 124 — POWER TO GET WEALTH

"The difference between being P.O.O.R. and being R.I.C.H. is being able to do G.O.O.D." - Rose Hall

Set goals to receive Residual Income that Creates Happiness so that you will have more money than those that Pass Over Opportunities Repeatedly. You will have more assets to Get Out Of Debt. Remember, God gives you power to attain wealth to sow seeds in the lives of others. This is so you will owe no man anything, but God's love.

_____

_____

_____

ABOUT THE AUTHOR

Rose Hall is a wife, mother of 4, a Health Professional and Entrepreneur. She loves reading, writing poetry, and serving her community.
Rose Hall
Winston-Salem, North Carolina
www.about.me/rosemhall
askrosehall@gmail.com
www.facebook.com/Destinations4u2

DAY 125 — HE IS A BURDEN BEARER

"So if the Son sets you free, you will be free indeed." - John 8:36 (NIV)

Walk with God in the freedom of forgiveness and He will remove the heavy load from you. Bury your heavy load at the foot of the cross while having hope in Jesus. Let His unconditional love free you from both your fears and your sins, as you relax in the light of His presence.

_____

_____

_____

ABOUT THE AUTHOR

Rose Hall is a wife, mother of 4, a Health Professional and Entrepreneur. She loves reading, writing poetry, and serving her community.
Rose Hall
Winston-Salem, North Carolina
www.about.me/rosemhall
askrosehall@gmail.com
www.facebook.com/Destinations4u2

DAY 126 – TRUST GOD

> "Trust in the LORD with all your heart and lean not on your own understanding." - Proverbs 3:5 (NIV)

Trust God here and now although He may be doing things you can't understand. Cling to His hands and find hope in Him because He is taking care of you. Refuse to obsess about your problems and how you are going to fix them just watch and see what He will do.

_____

_____

_____

ABOUT THE AUTHOR

Rose Hall is a wife, mother of 4, a Health Professional and Entrepreneur. She loves reading, writing poetry, and serving her community.
Rose Hall
Winston-Salem, North Carolina
www.about.me/rosemhall
askrosehall@gmail.com
www.facebook.com/Destinations4u2

DAY 127 — OH MY GOD! AKA OMG! PART 1

> "Now all glory to God, who is able, through his mighty power at work within us, to accomplish infinitely more than we might ask or think." - Ephesians 3:20 (NLT)

OMG! This is a phrase that we exclaim when something awesome happens or something catches us off guard or by surprise. I want to challenge you to think literally about this phrase. It says, "Oh My God!" We serve an amazing God that will bless us even when we don't deserve it or expect it. God will give us exceedingly, abundantly, more than you ask for or dream about. God is an OMG kind of God.

_____

_____

_____

ABOUT THE AUTHOR

Dr. Christine Handy is an educator, entrepreneur, and author. A respected high school principal and leader, she is also a Senior Manager with Send Out Cards and a leader with a health and wellness company. Additionally, she is a collaborating author in the Amazon Best Seller – Dear Fear Volume II.
Dr. Christine Handy
Germantown, Maryland
christine@aboveonly.ws
Facebook – https://www.facebook.com/chandy18

DAY 128 – OH MY GOD! AKA OMG! PART 2

"O give thanks unto the Lord; call upon his name: make known his deeds among the people." - Psalm 105:1 KJV

Take a moment to reflect on some of your blessings and just say out loud, "Oh My God!" Let's use this phrase to say thank you, to smile, to praise God for all of our blessings and miracles. Throw your hands up as you think about it and say, OMG! Text it, Tweet it! Put it on Facebook! Let's give God some glory on social media! Our God is an awesome God and deserves our praise. OMG! Shout on that!

_____

_____

_____

ABOUT THE AUTHOR

Dr. Christine Handy is an educator, entrepreneur, and author. A respected high school principal and leader, she is also a Senior Manager with Send Out Cards and a leader with a health and wellness company. Additionally, she is a collaborating author in the Amazon Best Seller – Dear Fear Volume II.
Dr. Christine Handy
Germantown, Maryland
christine@aboveonly.ws
Facebook – https://www.facebook.com/chandy18

DAY 129 – I AM PART 1

"I am the greatest!" - Muhammad Ali

People thought Muhammad Ali was pompous and full of himself. I do not believe this was true of Ali. He just spoke those things that were not as though they were, and soon it came to be. He is still one of the greatest boxers of all time. "I am" statements are powerful. Write your own. I am financially free, I am healthy, I am a size 10, I am happily married. Whatever you want in your life, just keep speaking it!

_____

_____

_____

ABOUT THE AUTHOR

Dr. Christine Handy is an educator, entrepreneur, and author. A respected high school principal and leader, she is also a Senior Manager with Send Out Cards and a leader with a health and wellness company. Additionally, she is a collaborating author in the Amazon Best Seller – Dear Fear Volume II.
Dr. Christine Handy
Germantown, Maryland
christine@aboveonly.ws
Facebook – https://www.facebook.com/chandy18

DAY 130 – I AM PART 2

"I am the light of the world!" - Jesus

The bible is filled with "I Am" statements and Jesus certainly utilized them often. Whatever comes behind these two words turns into a powerful affirmation. Talk to yourself in the morning. Say, I am beautiful, I am blessed, I am courageous, I am fearless, I am free, I am a leader, I am wealthy! When you start your day with positive affirmations, you are ready to receive all things positive. Try it today!

_____

_____

_____

ABOUT THE AUTHOR

Dr. Christine Handy is an educator, entrepreneur, and author. A respected high school principal and leader, she is also a Senior Manager with Send Out Cards and a leader with a health and wellness company. Additionally, she is a collaborating author in the Amazon Best Seller – Dear Fear Volume II.
Dr. Christine Handy
Germantown, Maryland
christine@aboveonly.ws
Facebook – https://www.facebook.com/chandy18

DAY 131 – AN ABUNDANCE MENTALITY

> "When you realize there is nothing lacking, the whole world belongs to you!" - Lao Tzu

Do you have a scarcity or an abundance mentality? Do you believe there is plenty of money to be made or do you believe there are limits? Do you believe in sharing what you know or are you going to keep it to yourself? When you move from a scarcity mentality to an abundance mentality, you are not thinking about lack, you believe that there are no limits and that everyone can get a piece of the pie. It's all about mindset!

_____

_____

_____

ABOUT THE AUTHOR

Dr. Christine Handy is an educator, entrepreneur, and author. A respected high school principal and leader, she is also a Senior Manager with Send Out Cards and a leader with a health and wellness company. Additionally, she is a collaborating author in the Amazon Best Seller – Dear Fear Volume II.
Dr. Christine Handy
Germantown, Maryland
christine@aboveonly.ws
Facebook – https://www.facebook.com/chandy18

DAY 132 – HAVE YOU LOST YOUR MIND?

"When you change your mind, you change the trajectory of your life!" - Dr. Christine Handy

A friend of mine is always saying, "Get your mind right!" If you want to change your life, you must first change your mind. If you want your finances to change, change how you think about money, how you save, how you spend, and how you use credit. Set your financial goals, lose your old mind about money, and don't stop until you are financially free.

_____

_____

_____

ABOUT THE AUTHOR

Dr. Christine Handy is an educator, entrepreneur, and author. A respected high school principal and leader, she is also a Senior Manager with Send Out Cards and a leader with a health and wellness company. Additionally, she is a collaborating author in the Amazon Best Seller – Dear Fear Volume II.
Dr. Christine Handy
Germantown, Maryland
christine@aboveonly.ws
Facebook – https://www.facebook.com/chandy18

DAY 133 – THE POWER OF MINDSET

"The Power of a Spiritual Mindset: Die Flesh, Die!!! Rise Holy Spirit, Rise!!!™" - Dr. Johni Cruse Craig

Life is a journey with many ups, downs, twist, and turns. Our core, "*our heart*" is the key component to how we react, respond, make decisions, and many other things as we journey. These internal factors have some very critical external implications in all areas of our lives. A true reflection inward is the beginning to an impactful transformation journey, which activates our divine *freedom* and *peace*!

ABOUT THE AUTHOR

Dr. Johni Cruse Craig is a Spirit on a Journey divinely purposed to serve as a Shifter, Educator, Strategist, Author, Encourager, & Transformational Life Coach.
www.hearttoheartservices.com
drjleray@hearttoheartservices.com
Johni Cruse Craig & Heart to Heart Services
Twitter: Dr. J. Le'Ray - @1PostitiveSpirit
Instagram: drjleray.heartcoach
LinkedIn: Dr. J. LeRay Cruse Craig

DAY 134 – THE POWER OF PERSPECTIVE

The POWER of perception to shift perspective leads to paradigm shifts.™ - Dr. Johni Cruse Craig

Our limited perception also limits our perspectives. Limited perspectives can stifle our ability to create wealth through financial freedom and develop our faith. It is when we are postured to hear and receive different perspectives that we can truly transform our minds and lead with amplified impact. As we journey and ascend with this perspective, our vision becomes more defined allowing us to serve in our divine purpose.

_____

_____

_____

ABOUT THE AUTHOR

Dr. Johni Cruse Craig is a Spirit on a Journey divinely purposed to serve as a Shifter, Educator, Strategist, Author, Encourager, & Transformational Life Coach.
www.hearttoheartservices.com
drjleray@hearttoheartservices.com
Johni Cruse Craig & Heart to Heart Services
Twitter: Dr. J. Le'Ray - @1PostitiveSpirit
Instagram: drjleray.heartcoach
LinkedIn: Dr. J. LeRay Cruse Craig

DAY 135 – THE POWER OF YOUR STORY: YOU ARE AN EDUCATOR

"Education: It's A Heart Matter®" - Dr. Johni Cruse Craig

Everybody is an educator. An authentic heart allows the fire from within to reignite, reset and fuel other hearts with that internal passion. Education, be it formal or informal, is necessary to build wealth and financial freedom. It is imperative that each of us boldly and confidently open our mouths to share our stories to educate and further awaken others. Our life can serve as the content for our teachings.

_____

_____

_____

ABOUT THE AUTHOR

Dr. Johni Cruse Craig is a Spirit on a Journey divinely purposed to serve as a Shifter, Educator, Strategist, Author, Encourager, & Transformational Life Coach.
www.hearttoheartservices.com
drjleray@hearttoheartservices.com
Johni Cruse Craig & Heart to Heart Services
Twitter: Dr. J. Le'Ray - @1PostitiveSpirit
Instagram: drjleray.heartcoach
LinkedIn: Dr. J. LeRay Cruse Craig

DAY 136 — THE POWER OF UNITY

"For there is one body and one Spirit, just as you have been called to one glorious hope for the future." - Ephesians 4:4 NLT

As spirits on a journey, we are one and are commissioned to journey accordingly. Understanding this fact manifest accelerated peace, provision, purpose and impact. We all are pressing towards the mark and when we discover who and whose we are, serving in our rightful position is not hard work, it is heart work. Our gifts were ordained and it is our responsibility to discover, develop and activate them for kingdom advancement.

_____

_____

_____

ABOUT THE AUTHOR

Dr. Johni Cruse Craig is a Spirit on a Journey divinely purposed to serve as a Shifter, Educator, Strategist, Author, Encourager, & Transformational Life Coach.
www.hearttoheartservices.com
drjleray@hearttoheartservices.com
Johni Cruse Craig & Heart to Heart Services
Twitter: Dr. J. Le'Ray - @1PostitiveSpirit
Instagram: drjleray.heartcoach
LinkedIn: Dr. J. LeRay Cruse Craig

DAY 137 – HOPE THAT OVERCOMES

"The eyes of your understanding being enlightened; that you may know what is the hope of His calling, what are the riches of the glory of His inheritance in the saints". -Ephesians 1:18 (NKJ)

As the Holy Spirit lights the way, we may find ourselves facing soul blocks. We go through life, carrying emotions, decisions, and relationships, fumbling, while juggling the weight of these soul blocks, like heavy stones. As the Lord reveals lies, and woundedness, through the cross, we find the freedom by letting go because our hope is in Christ. This season equips us to be the overcomer he has called us to be.

_____

_____

_____

ABOUT THE AUTHOR

Laurie Marks Vincent
Speaker, Author, Singer-Songwriter
The Lord has set her ministry apart with messages that reveal faith principles, her music, and a testimony of miraculous healing.
LMVministry.com
bookings@LMVministry.com
http://www.facebook.com/LMVministry
Instragram: @laurieMvincent

DAY 138 – YOUR DESTINY

"He who calls you is faithful; he will surely do it." - 1 Thessalonians 5:24 (ESV)

Take comfort in knowing that he will not fail you. He cannot fail you because he is God and he does not lie. He has called you and anointed you with gifts. He has planned every good work for you to do and he desires you to use your gifts to create change for his glory (Eph 2:10). As you seek him, your destiny awaits. He will surely do it!

_____

_____

_____

ABOUT THE AUTHOR

Laurie Marks Vincent
Speaker, Author, Singer-Songwriter
The Lord has set her ministry apart with messages that reveal faith principles, her music, and a testimony of miraculous healing.
LMVministry.com
bookings@LMVministry.com
http://www.facebook.com/LMVministry
Instragram: @laurieMvincent

DAY 139 – WINGS TO VICTORY

"(He) who satisfies you with good so that your youth is renewed like the eagle's."
- Psalm 103:5

In the 13th year of a long struggle with my health, I was finally diagnosed with Fibromyalgia, Chronic Fatigue, and Depression. Through this, God brought revelation, teaching me many faith principals. This very scripture catapulted my faith. I confessed every day regardless of my circumstances or feelings. Then, the Lord miraculously and instantaneously healed me. He has proven his faithfulness. His Word is life, that increases faith, moves mountains and brings miracles.

_____

_____

_____

ABOUT THE AUTHOR

Laurie Marks Vincent
Speaker, Author, Singer-Songwriter
The Lord has set her ministry apart with messages that reveal faith principles, her music, and a testimony of miraculous healing.
LMVministry.com
bookings@LMVministry.com
http://www.facebook.com/LMVministry
Instragram: @laurieMvincent

DAY 140 – OVER MY HEAD

"Set your minds on things that are above, not on things that are on earth." - Colossians 3:2

When life is hard, our perspective may be faulty. We're so used to sinking that It's hard to believe that God has a better plan. We may even believe that we are cursed. Scripture tells us we should be Kingdom focused. When we change our thinking, it will positively affect our circumstances. As a child of the King, we inherit from the Kingdom above, that which changes our circumstances here on the earth.

_____

_____

_____

ABOUT THE AUTHOR

Laurie Marks Vincent
Speaker, Author, Singer-Songwriter
The Lord has set her ministry apart with messages that reveal faith principles, her music, and a testimony of miraculous healing.
LMVministry.com
bookings@LMVministry.com
http://www.facebook.com/LMVministry
Instragram: @laurieMvincent

DAY 141 – GOD'S BLUEPRINTS

"Without counsel plans fail, but with many advisers they succeed."- Proverbs 15:22 (ESV)

The rules for success are simple and basic. Failing to create a plan while seeking the steps that bring the desired results will not bring success. Ask friends and professionals as you seek God's leading. You don't know who God will speak through. When you hear the words that fire-up your passion and help you see clearly God's blueprints for you, then you will surely know. You can do this!

_____

_____

_____

ABOUT THE AUTHOR

Laurie Marks Vincent
Speaker, Author, Singer-Songwriter
The Lord has set her ministry apart with messages that reveal faith principles, her music, and a testimony of miraculous healing.
LMVministry.com
bookings@LMVministry.com
http://www.facebook.com/LMVministry
Instragram: @laurieMvincent

DAY 142 – SHOULDERS LIKE BLADES

"As iron sharpens iron, so one person sharpens another." - Proverbs 27:17

Conflicts are not to be avoided. You're frustrated and you felt the friction. Where does the blade fall? It falls on the iron. It's that place in the heart sharpened by the revelation of wisdom and truth. God uses others to strengthen us, but also to sharpen our spiritual growth. We're rubbing shoulders! We should also desire to be like iron in the lives of others, being a positive and compassionate influence.

_____

_____

_____

ABOUT THE AUTHOR

Laurie Marks Vincent
Speaker, Author, Singer-Songwriter
The Lord has set her ministry apart with messages that reveal faith principles, her music, and a testimony of miraculous healing.
LMVministry.com
bookings@LMVministry.com
http://www.facebook.com/LMVministry
Instragram: @laurieMvincent

DAY 143 — THE BEST SEAT IN THE HOUSE

"For he raised us from the dead along with Christ and seated us with him in the heavenly realms because we are united with Christ Jesus." - Ephesians 2:6

Christ now sits next to the Father, and we are seated with him in the heavenly realms. The heavenly realm is a whole new country. We now have access to the throne of God. Every work that Jesus did on the cross for our healing, provision, salvation, and victory is complete, redeemed on the cross and made available through him. We have a lifetime pass to the best seat in the house.

_____

_____

_____

ABOUT THE AUTHOR

Laurie Marks Vincent
Speaker, Author, Singer-Songwriter
The Lord has set her ministry apart with messages that reveal faith principles, her music, and a testimony of miraculous healing.
LMVministry.com
bookings@LMVministry.com
http://www.facebook.com/LMVministry
Instragram: @laurieMvincent

DAY 144 – BE LIGHT

"You are the light of the world. A city set on a hill cannot be hidden." - Matthew 5:14

Jesus said in John 8:12 that he is the Light of the World. In Christ, we are also light, reflecting his light and love to a dark world. People look for hope and seek light but they wander because Satan comes as an angel of light to deceive. In every deed, every place you go and every word you say, stand tall on your hill. Let others see his light amidst the darkness.

_____

_____

_____

ABOUT THE AUTHOR

Laurie Marks Vincent
Speaker, Author, Singer-Songwriter
The Lord has set her ministry apart with messages that reveal faith principles, her music, and a testimony of miraculous healing.
LMVministry.com
bookings@LMVministry.com
http://www.facebook.com/LMVministry
Instragram: @laurieMvincent

DAY 145 – THE OXEN'S YOKE

> "For my yoke is easy and my burden is light." - Matthew 11:30

When a young ox is being trained to plow the field, he pulls a "yoke" that is placed on his shoulders, alongside a more experienced ox. This helps the young ox gain strength and understanding as the more experienced ox bares the load. Jesus compares our burdens to the ox's yoke. He will walk beside you and bare the load of your burden, as you trust him and follow his lead.

_____

_____

_____

ABOUT THE AUTHOR

Laurie Marks Vincent
Speaker, Author, Singer-Songwriter
The Lord has set her ministry apart with messages that reveal faith principles, her music, and a testimony of miraculous healing.
LMVministry.com
bookings@LMVministry.com
http://www.facebook.com/LMVministry
Instragram: @laurieMvincent

DAY 146 – SURRENDERED

"You shall have no other gods before me." - Deuteronomy 5:7

Obedience to God is a choice that is moved by our love for him and the power of his grace working in our life. Every day, in all that we do, is it an act of worship unto him? In the end, does all that we do honor and reflect him? Anything else placed above him, indicates a place of our heart that is not likely surrendered to the Lord.

_____

_____

_____

ABOUT THE AUTHOR

Laurie Marks Vincent
Speaker, Author, Singer-Songwriter
The Lord has set her ministry apart with messages that reveal faith principles, her music, and a testimony of miraculous healing.
LMVministry.com
bookings@LMVministry.com
http://www.facebook.com/LMVministry
Instragram: @laurieMvincent

DAY 147 – THE SEED OF FAITH

"Now faith is the assurance of things hoped for, the conviction of things not seen." - Hebrews 11:1

The Mustard Seed is the only seed that cannot be grafted with another seed. It is the same with your faith. You cannot mix faith with doubt, fear, worry or anything else. Remove doubt or other bad seeds, by watering your faith with promises from the Word of God. Only absolute faith assures you with hope and confidence, to receive from God, what is not seen but is already yours.

_____

_____

_____

ABOUT THE AUTHOR

Laurie Marks Vincent
Speaker, Author, Singer-Songwriter
The Lord has set her ministry apart with messages that reveal faith principles, her music, and a testimony of miraculous healing.
LMVministry.com
bookings@LMVministry.com
http://www.facebook.com/LMVministry
Instragram: @laurieMvincent

DAY 148 – HOW THE BLESSINGS FLOW

"Give generously to him and do so without a grudging heart; then because of this the Lord your God will bless you in all your work and in everything you put your hand to." - Deuteronomy 15:10

Although our heart may be moved, fear of not having enough causes our hands to close. As a result, we can't be a blessing to God or others. We're also not able to receive blessings from God that he so desires to give us. We must first sow, for blessings to flow. When your heart and hands are open, God's blessings will flow through you and to you.

_____

_____

_____

ABOUT THE AUTHOR

Laurie Marks Vincent
Speaker, Author, Singer-Songwriter
The Lord has set her ministry apart with messages that reveal faith principles, her music, and a testimony of miraculous healing.
LMVministry.com
bookings@LMVministry.com
http://www.facebook.com/LMVministry
Instragram: @laurieMvincent

DAY 149 – BROKEN AND BEAUTIFUL

"Instead of your shame there shall be a double portion; instead of dishonor they shall rejoice in their lot; therefore in their land they shall possess a double portion; they shall have everlasting joy." - Isaiah 61:7

God uses broken things to reveal his beauty. Rain comes from clouds that break open. Seeds break under the earth to yield a bloom and give us a harvest in due season. God will turn your brokenness into something beautiful. What you thought was meant for your demise, will prove that with Christ, you will thrive. He will turn your brokenness into a victory story and use you for his glory.

_____

_____

_____

ABOUT THE AUTHOR

Laurie Marks Vincent
Speaker, Author, Singer-Songwriter
The Lord has set her ministry apart with messages that reveal faith principles, her music, and a testimony of miraculous healing.
LMVministry.com
bookings@LMVministry.com
http://www.facebook.com/LMVministry
Instragram: @laurieMvincent

DAY 150 – DECLUTTERING THE MIND PART 1

"Self-care is important. When you take time to replenish your spirit, it allows you to serve others from the overflow. You cannot serve from an empty vessel."
- Eleanor Brown

We all want to live our best lives. We set goals, dream big, and make plans to be the best version of ourselves. We write on mirrors, journal and use planners. But are we also taking the time to declutter our minds? To evolve into our best selves, we must take the time to deal with emotional and mental baggage. Self-care is an integral part of your personal development.

_____

_____
_____

_____

ABOUT THE AUTHOR

Tarasha Lloyd
Jacksonville, North Carolina
Facebook - @lloydconsultingcompany
https://lloydconsulting34.wixsite.com/mysite-1
tarasha3434@gmail.com

DAY 151 – DECLUTTERING THE MIND PART 2

"Self-care is important. When you take time to replenish your spirit, it allows you to serve others from the overflow. You cannot serve from an empty vessel."
- Eleanor Brown

Here's my one of best personal tips: Guided meditation is key component to daily my success. In conjunction with praying and journaling, I am able to process my thoughts and feelings and rid myself of negativity. I invite every woman to incorporate at least five to ten minutes a day to search social video channels, still their minds and spend this time to rejuvenate mind, body and spirit. You cannot run effectively on junk - and that includes a cluttered mind.

_____

_____

_____

ABOUT THE AUTHOR

Tarasha Lloyd
Jacksonville, North Carolina
Facebook - @lloydconsultingcompany
https://lloydconsulting34.wixsite.com/mysite-1
tarasha3434@gmail.com

DAY 152 – GRACED TO WIN PART 1

"Poised, Positioned, and Powerful!" - Catherine Green

We are graced to win. The trials and tribulations you have endured throughout the years have cultivated a winner inside of you. The champion within have weathered the storms of every season. So stand poised, positioned, and powerful, after you have done all. Champions cross dimensional borders and break generational curses. Be strong and of good courage, you have, will, and shall overcome whatever life may bring.

_____

_____

_____

ABOUT THE AUTHOR

Catherine Green is a phenomenal woman of God. She ministers truth in her region and answers the call to nations to release joy and awaken dry bones.
Catherine Green
Homewood, Illinois
jicgreen05@yahoo.com
www.facebook.com/catheine.green.92754
https://twitter.com/4yourglorylife?s=09

DAY 153 – GRACED TO WIN PART 2

"Poised, Positioned, and Powerful!" - Catherine Green

What you went through did not kill you because you have purpose inside of you. It is time for champions to rise and shine. There is something only you can create, build, and do in the earth that nobody can duplicate, alter, or change. Leave a lifelong legacy of hope by making your mark. Live the dream. We have been graced to win in life while being poised, positioned, and powerful!

_____

_____

_____

ABOUT THE AUTHOR

Catherine Green is a phenomenal woman of God. She ministers truth in her region and answers the call to nations to release joy and awaken dry bones.
Catherine Green
Homewood, Illinois
jicgreen05@yahoo.com
www.facebook.com/catheine.green.92754
https://twitter.com/4yourglorylife?s=09

DAY 154 – BE ANXIOUS FOR NOTHING

"Do not be anxious about anything, but in every situation, by prayer and petition, with thanksgiving, present your requests to God." - Philippians 4:6

Throughout my life, I have realized that worry brings on dis-ease. I had to give it to the Lord. No longer will I suffer at the hands of being anxious. I have been in the hospital several times because I thought I could fix all things by myself. After the third time of being hospitalized, I came to my end and that was the time I allowed God to work in and through me. Now, He works and I relax. He can handle it.

_____

_____

_____

ABOUT THE AUTHOR

Greta Ann Belasco Murray
Orlando, Florida
gretaannbelasco@yahoo.com
www.beautybygreta.neora.com

171

DAY 155 – HOPE FOR STRENGTH

"But those who wait on the Lord shall renew their strength; They shall mount up with wings like eagles, they shall run and not be weary, they shall walk and not faint." - Isaiah 40:31

As a maturing Christian, I have had to recite this verse many times. Losing my brother and mother in consecutive years was very painful. We all know everyone has to die but it does not lessen the pain of losing a loved one when it happens. Having my faith and hoping in the Lord for strength each day is what brought me through those hard times. I am a living witness that his promises are true.

_____

_____

_____

ABOUT THE AUTHOR

Greta Ann Belasco Murray
Orlando, Florida
gretaannbelasco@yahoo.com
www.beautybygreta.neora.com

DAY 156 — OBJECTS ARE CLOSER THAN THEY APPEAR

"It doesn't matter how slow you go as long as you don't stop." - Confucius

Exhaustion, weariness and frustration are compelling and real distractions. When these set in, you feel physically ill. It's extremely easy for one thing to "pluck your last nerve." The common response is that you want to give up, to quit. However, where will that leave you? Don't stop, even if you have to drop down to a crawl. Keep going. A new day will bring new energy and a new opportunity. When that new day comes, you will awake to see that you are now closer to your goal.

_____

_____

_____

ABOUT THE AUTHOR

Nicole Rischilde Bramwell, MD, MBA
Married~Mother of inspiring Daughter
Entrepreneur~Speaker~Author~Physician 20+yrs
Antiaging & Wellness Consultant
Creator of Healthy Curves by CFIWeightLoss.com
Apopka, Florida
www.cfiweightloss.com
drbweightlossmd@gmail.com
www.facebook.com/CFIWeightManagement

DAY 157 – WATERING YOUR SOUL

"There is a sacredness in tears. They are not the mark of weakness, but of power. They speak more eloquently than ten thousand tongues. They are the messengers of overwhelming grief, of deep contrition and of unspeakable joy."
- Washington Irving

A friend of mine told me she isn't going to church because she cries every time she goes. Why is crying considered bad or shameful? Why don't boys cry? God created an intricate system for tears, it's purpose must be grand. Tears are from deep within to soothe broken hearts, release immense pain and to allow joy to burst out of us and onto others. It's my party, and I'll cry if I want to!

_____

_____

_____

ABOUT THE AUTHOR

Nicole Rischilde Bramwell, MD, MBA
Married~Mother of inspiring Daughter
Entrepreneur~Speaker~Author~Physician 20+yrs
Antiaging & Wellness Consultant
Creator of Healthy Curves by CFIWeightLoss.com
Apopka, Florida
www.cfiweightloss.com
drbweightlossmd@gmail.com
www.facebook.com/CFIWeightManagement

DAY 158 – FIRE WALKING

"When you pass through the waters, I will be with you; and through the rivers, they shall not overflow you. When you walk through the fire, you shall not be burned, nor shall the flame scorch you." - Isaiah 43:2

Have you ever felt like you are drowning at the same time as walking on hot coals? I have felt this way too many times to count. Despite how hot it had gotten or how "in over my head" I felt, my faithful God helped me go through these moments with incredible victory. When I have no more reserve, I stand on my "mustard seed" of faith. God stands with me and moves on my behalf.

_____

_____

_____

ABOUT THE AUTHOR

Nicole Bramwell, MD, MBA
Apopka, Florida
www.cfiweightloss.com
drbweightlossmd@gmail.com
www.facebook.com/CFIWeightManagement

DAY 159 – STEADY YOURSELF

"To console those who mourn in Zion, to give them beauty for ashes, the oil of joy for mourning, the garment of praise for the spirit of heaviness, that they may be called trees of righteousness, the planting of the Lord, that He may be glorified." - Isaiah 61:3

We have all been on shaky ground, where we felt so unsteady. In such a time, we are grabbing for something solid and rooted. The Lord is our rock. He is the firmly planted tree that we can hang onto knowing. He has us covered, enfolded, and lifted up in all things. Who else, but God, can give us wondrous beauty for the nothingness of ashes?!

_____

_____

_____

ABOUT THE AUTHOR

Nicole Bramwell, MD, MBA
Apopka, Florida
www.cfiweightloss.com
drbweightlossmd@gmail.com
www.facebook.com/CFIWeightManagement

DAY 160 – PROCRASTINATION FOR PERFECTION IS PARENT TO PARALYSIS

"You don't have to be great to get started, but you have to get started to be great."
- Les Brown

Dream, pray, hope and dream some more. Extreme passion for our dreams can sometimes paralyze us. This is especially true when fear, ridicule, doubt, and previous failures infiltrate our minds. We then project the low expectations others have for themselves onto ourselves. Dreams without action will soon be forgotten. Take any step toward your dream however wobbly or imperfect. You will move closer to your dream with the next step forward.

_____

_____

_____

ABOUT THE AUTHOR

Nicole Bramwell, MD, MBA
Apopka, Florida
www.cfiweightloss.com
drbweightlossmd@gmail.com
www.facebook.com/CFIWeightManagement

DAY 161 – RESPONSIBILITY IS POWER NOT BLAME

"Brokenness is for a season, but lessons from it are for a lifetime." - Priscilla Shirer

Injustice has a way of knocking you off balance. You create false beliefs about yourself on the flawed foundational belief you adopted from others. This happens in every type of relationship, within the legal system, in your professional life, and in your community. My own creation of being in a state of overwhelm catapulted me into a situation that rocked my world. I collided with realms I never would have imagined. The overwhelm blunted my ability and capacity to hear my own intuition. As a result, I did not decide who I was but rather, I allowed others to define my identity. This is a common theme for women. My story is not of victimhood or unfairness. This is my journey, my life lesson for me to take responsibility for myself, to expand and be powerful. My life lesson is to be brave and powerful in your own identity through Christ.

ABOUT THE AUTHOR

Nicole Bramwell, MD, MBA
Apopka, Florida
www.cfiweightloss.com
drbweightlossmd@gmail.com
www.facebook.com/CFIWeightManagement

DAY 162 – BE OF RIGHT MIND

"Finally brethren, whatever things are true, whatever things are noble, whatever things are just, whatever things are pure, whatever things are lovely, whatever things are of good report, if there is any virtue and if there is anything noteworthy - meditate on these things." - Philippians 4:8

Throughout life you can take the easy way out. They say "everyone does it that way," "that's good enough," "You did more than most," or "they don't appreciate what you're doing." The right thing will likely not be the easy or perfect thing. The noble and just thing to do is inside of God's character, reflected in you through your words and actions. What do you do when no one is watching?

_____

_____

_____

ABOUT THE AUTHOR

Nicole Bramwell, MD, MBA
Apopka, Florida
www.cfiweightloss.com
drbweightlossmd@gmail.com
www.facebook.com/CFIWeightManagement

DAY 163 – HIS HAND IS UPON HER

"To the end that my glory may sing praise to You and not be silent. O Lord my God, I will give thanks to you forever." - Psalm 30:12

At age two, our daughter was abandoned in a daycare bathroom during a fire drill. Traumatized, her speech was stunted and a learning disability was diagnosed. She did all therapies without complaint and she remained joyful.

My husband and I struggled, though. We argued and cried; we trusted and prayed. To see her now, you would never know what she has been through! His light in her shines to His glory and God kept us preserved as a family.

_____

_____

_____

ABOUT THE AUTHOR

Nicole Bramwell, MD, MBA
Apopka, Florida
www.cfiweightloss.com
drbweightlossmd@gmail.com
www.facebook.com/CFIWeightManagement

DAY 164 – FAITH IS A LIFELINE

"Where two or three are gathered together in My name, I am there in the midst of them." - Matthew 18:20

Life has taken me to places that felt like hell itself. After two years of trying to give birth, plus an operation and with medication, I was told that my daughter was dead in my womb. My doctor said "we" will pray. Ten days later, our baby girl couldn't wait to show off with her miracle birth! She lives!

God is faithful to His promises. When you don't know, don't

understand or you feel lost - hold on. He is with you.

_____

_____

_____

ABOUT THE AUTHOR

Nicole Bramwell, MD, MBA
Apopka, Florida
www.cfiweightloss.com
drbweightlossmd@gmail.com
www.facebook.com/CFIWeightManagement

DAY 165 — BEING UNAFRAID OF THE UNKNOWN

"If one advances confidently in the direction of his dreams, and endeavors to live the life which he has imagined, he will meet with success unexpected in common   hours."
- Henry David Thoreau

I have been told, on more than one occasion, that I am an oddball. I do not take it as a negative slight against me. What I hear, instead is, "you do unexpected things that brings me joy." I know that God made me different and He expects me to show others my light. I step out on my faith into the unknown to achieve what God has for me.

_____

_____

_____

ABOUT THE AUTHOR

Dahlia Ashford, Life Coach and Independent Educational Consultant, and CEO/Founder of Transform. Evolve. Transcend., LLC. Dahlia Ashford
Greensboro, North Carolina
www.evolvetranscend.com
transformetranscendllc@gmail.com
Facebook: Transform. Evolve. Transcend., LLC
Twitter: @DAshford2018 | Instagram: dahliaashford

DAY 166 – TAKE YOUR TIME GOD IS IN CONTROL

"It does not matter how slowly you go as long as you do not stop." - Confucius

I must remind myself daily that God is in control. He does not want me to rush through life, but to enjoy and experience His wonders. I take time to speak with people and give them a friendly smile. When you do not rush through life, I find that experience teaches me more than any educational institution. Take time to meditate, read your bible, or check in with a dear friend.

_____

_____

_____

ABOUT THE AUTHOR

Dahlia Ashford, Life Coach and Independent Educational Consultant, and CEO/Founder of Transform. Evolve. Transcend., LLC.
Dahlia Ashford
Greensboro, North Carolina
www.evolvetranscend.com
transformetranscendllc@gmail.com
Facebook: Transform. Evolve. Transcend., LLC
Twitter: @DAshford2018
Instagram: dahliaashford

DAY 167 — FREE TO BE UNAPOLOGETICALLY ME

"Be fearless in the pursuit of what sets your soul on fire" - Unknown

In over fourty years, I have tried, succeeded and failed countless times. I was too busy being a "jack of all trades" and a "master of none." Following the wide path to get rich schemes that ultimately never flourished into anything meaningful. I was a passionate event planner and florist. Yet, something even more worthwhile was peeking through beyond these two industries. What truly sets my soul on fire is unapologetically being me. I absolutely love empowering, innovating, mentoring, writing, slaying goals, and being brave, all while being very afraid. Fear is not a deal stopper for me.

_____

_____

_____

ABOUT THE AUTHOR

Tartanita Nowell, a native of Charleston, SC. Author|SheO and Visionary of 'Stilettos & Business Plans®"|Purpose Coach|Mentor|Goal Strategist
Charleston, South Carolina
stbpnetwork@gmail.com
https://www.facebook.com/tanita.nowell.7

DAY 168 — GOT PURPOSE?

"With hope, I breathe; With purpose, I live." - Tartanita Nowell

Are you just breathing or or are you living? If you are living, are you living your purpose? This is the purpose God created and chose you to bring to fruition.

Are you laboring in vain or laboring for birth? If you are still laboring (hoping), the contractions (purpose) are strengthening and the wait is almost over. Simply inhale with faith and exhale with excellence. All that is left to do is to give birth! Achieve your goals with one breath at a time with hope. This will keep your life filled with purpose!

_____

_____

_____

ABOUT THE AUTHOR

Tartanita Nowell, a native of Charleston, SC. Author|SheO and Visionary of 'Stilettos & Business Plans®"|Purpose Coach|Mentor|Goal Strategist
Charleston, South Carolina
stbpnetwork@gmail.com
https://www.facebook.com/tanita.nowell.7

DAY 169 — NO BATTERIES REQUIRED

"And He said to me, My grace is sufficient for you, for My strength is made perfect in weakness." - 2 Corinthians 12:9

When you think you can't, you can. When you are weary, you can find strength. When you are unsure, you can with security in God. Through the tears, you can. In your weakness God's strength is made perfect. This way God gets all the glory, and you get to say, 'Look what the Lord has done!'

_____

_____

_____

ABOUT THE AUTHOR

Dr. Sherman is a Wife, Mother, Grandmother, Prophetess, Author, Co- Author, Chancellor/Founder of Ramah Institute of Theology who was chosen to honor President Barack Obama, First Lady Michelle Obama and 65th Sec. of State Gen. Colin Luther Powell; Senior Pastor-Harvest Time International Ministry; Founder-Issachar Institute of Prophets and Apostles; Founder of CDC Ministry Fellowship.
Apostle Dr. Carol J. Sherman
Senior Pastor
www.drcarol.org
Drcsm3@gmail.com

DAY 170 — FULLY-LOADED

"Before I formed you in the womb, I knew you; before you were born, I sanctified you; I ordained you a prophet to the nations." - Jeremiah 1:5

What a destiny! You came to earth fully-loaded. God has spoken over your life, sanctified you, and declared your purpose! Everything you need is already inside of you. All you need is to access the confidence of your identity and walk in it!

_____

_____

_____

ABOUT THE AUTHOR

Dr. Sherman is a Wife, Mother, Grandmother, Prophetess, Author, Co-Author, Chancellor/Founder of Ramah Institute of Theology who was chosen to honor President Barack Obama, First Lady Michelle Obama and 65th Sec. of State Gen. Colin Luther Powell; Senior Pastor-Harvest Time International Ministry; Founder-Issachar Institute of Prophets and Apostles; Founder of CDC Ministry Fellowship.
Apostle Dr. Carol J. Sherman
Senior Pastor
www.drcarol.org
Drcsm3@gmail.com

DAY 171 – UNDO PAST WOUNDS QUICKLY

> "When you forgive, you in no way change the past – but you sure do change the future." - Bernard Metzler

I once heard that we spend the first half of our life dealing with childhood wounds and the second half undoing them. Instead of fighting these wounds, embrace them. Everything in life is an experience. They are neither good nor bad. They are only experiences. So be grateful for these experiences because they made you who you are today. Express gratitude for them. You are whole and perfect.

_____

_____

_____

ABOUT THE AUTHOR

Pat Knauer
Corner Office University, Tridap Meda
www.cornerofficeuniversity.com,
https://tridapmedia.com
pat@cornerofficeuniversity.com
https://www.facebook.com/pat.schoofknauer

DAY 172 — DEMAND WHAT YOU WANT

"The universe doesn't give you what you ask for with your thoughts; it gives you what you demand with your actions." - Steve Maraboli

Intention is the fuel of your dreams. When you have a vision so clear that you know, without a doubt, what the end result is, you act and behave as if it is already done. You get into alignment with your vision. And when the Universe/God/Spirit gets the signal that it is already done, it scrambles to catch up to you - to make it happen.

_____

_____

_____

ABOUT THE AUTHOR

Pat Knauer
Corner Office University, Tridap Meda
www.cornerofficeuniversity.com,
https://tridapmedia.com
pat@cornerofficeuniversity.com
https://www.facebook.com/pat.schoofknauer

DAY 173 — BE SATISFIED

"I am the sum total of what I have been confessing through the years." - Joel Osteen

We must be careful of what we allow to escape from our lips. May we speak words of the long life that God has promised us. People have prophesied their own deaths by the words they have spoken. One such person is Anna Nicole Smith, who predicted that she would probably die at age 37. She died at age 39. May you be blessed with long life.

_____

_____

_____

ABOUT THE AUTHOR

Barbara Johnson
Orlando, Florida
Barbiedoll71@hotmail.com
Getyourglowon.neora.com

DAY 174 — WHO ARE YOU REALLY?

"But you are a chosen generation, a royal priesthood, a holy nation, His own special people, that you may proclaim the praises of Him who called you out of darkness into His marvelous light" - 1 Peter 2:9

It has taken decades of my life to finally accept and come to terms with who I am. Once I decided to believe what God says about me, heard it repeatedly and got it into my spirit, I acted like the royalty that I truly am. Belief is powerful. May your belief in who God says you are take root in your spirit and spring into life.

_____

_____

_____

ABOUT THE AUTHOR

Barbara Johnson
Orlando, Florida
Barbiedoll71@hotmail.com
Getyourglowon.neora.com

DAY 175 – THE BUMPS IN THE ROAD OF LIFE

"I've told you all this so that trusting me, you will be unshakable and assured, deeply at peace. In this godless world you will continue to experience difficulties. But take heart! I've conquered the world." - John 16:33

In life there will always be bumps in the road and God tells us he will never leave nor forsake us. We must understand that speed bumps were placed in the road to slow us down. The speed bumps of life can nearly bring us to a complete stop, but your faith in God will give you the wisdom to navigate more wisely over the speed bumps. So, just slow down, get out of your own way, and let God.

_____

_____

_____

ABOUT THE AUTHOR

Minister Redd-Latimer is a wife, mother, women of God, coach, mentor, harvester, entrepreneur and founder of Reaching the Mark for Today's Youths. Her goal is to Inspire young people. She often says, "I want someone to look at me and say," because of you I didn't give up.""
Minister Michelle Redd-Latimer
Boyds, Maryland
thefutureisyours@live.com
Facebook – Coach Michelle Redd-Latimer

DAY 176 – FORWARD NOT BACKWARD

"They followed the stubborn inclinations of their evil hearts. They went backwards and not forward." - Jeremiah 7:24

The Apostle Paul was full of fire in his everyday life. Adopt this same attitude every morning. Shake off the ashes of yesterday's disappointment. Say to yourself, 'I'm not looking back.'

I can encourage you. Your friends can even cheer you on, but no one can put God's fire in your soul. Your fire will come when you 'put your foot down' and make a decision to move forward with God.

_____

_____

_____

ABOUT THE AUTHOR

Lavette Gulley, CNA
Orlando, Florida
serenitycompanionservices@yahoo.com
www.linkedin.com/in/lavette-d-gulley-4ba13b42

DAY 177 – ALLOW GOD TO CLEAR THE WAY

"A fire was kindled in their company, the flame burned up the wicked." - Psalm 106:18

The Israelites quickly forgot what God had done for them because they focused on their own discouraging words and thoughts. God still forgave them. Forgive yourself. Throw away your rearview mirror. Stop looking back at mistakes, mistreatment, and discouragement. Decide not to look to the left nor to the right. Keep looking straight ahead. God isn't looking at your past, nor should you. Move forward, God has plans for you ahead.

_____

_____

_____

ABOUT THE AUTHOR

Lavette Gulley, CNA
Orlando, Florida
serenitycompanionservices@yahoo.com
www.linkedin.com/in/lavette-d-gulley-4ba13b42

DAY 178 – GOD WILL USE THIS FOR GOOD

"For I know the plans I have for you," says the Lord. "They ae plans for good and not for disaster; to give you a future and a hope." - Jeremiah 29:11 NLT

Countless stories in the Bible demonstrate God taking what was meant for bad and using it for good. Joseph was thrown into a pit. God took him from the pit to the palace! What is your pit encounter? We are overwhelmed with situations that appear to be evil and sometimes they are evil! God specializes in turning tests into testimonies. Remember His promise that He will use it for your good.

_____

_____

_____

ABOUT THE AUTHOR

Chinita Irby, Mother, Amazon Best-Selling Author, Dear Fear Volume 2, Educator, and Independent Business Owner at Total Life Changes.
Selma, Alabama
https://shop.totallifechanges.com/chinitairby
chinitairby@gmail.com
https://www.facebook.com/healthandwealthinalabama/

DAY 179 – TRUSTING GOD ON A DAILY BASIS

Jesus said: "If you then, being evil, know how to give good gifts to your children, how much more will your Father who is in heaven give good things to those who ask Him!" - Matthew 7:11

It is difficult to trust when we have an estranged relationship with our earthly father. Our Heavenly Father is not man. He longs to give us our heart's desires. He knows what we need before we ask of Him. He knows our end from the beginning. He also knows the in between. Trust God through the process and know that He is a present help when we have trouble. Abba Father says surrender it all to Him.

_____

_____

_____

ABOUT THE AUTHOR

Chinita Irby, Mother, Amazon Best-Selling Author, Dear Fear Volume 2, Educator, and Independent Business Owner at Total Life Changes.
Selma, Alabama
https://shop.totallifechanges.com/chinitairby
chinitairby@gmail.com
https://www.facebook.com/healthandwealthinalabama/

DAY 180 – YOUR DIVINE BODY

"A person's health isn't generally a reflection of genes, but how their environment is influencing them. Genes are the direct cause of less than 1% of diseases: 99% is how we respond to the world." - Dr. Bruce Lipton

The body is designed to heal itself. All you need to do is provide your body with an environment that allows your immune system to do what it is designed to do. That means the food you eat, the thoughts you think, the emotions you feel, the people you surround yourself with will either build you up or tear you down. What environment do you want to create for your body?

_____

_____

_____

ABOUT THE AUTHOR

Karin Weiri, LMFT, Therapist, Break Through Life Coach, Speaker, Radio Talk Show Host
Orange City, Florida
Insights Counseling Center, Inc.
www.insightscounselingcenter.com
www.insightsblissfulretreats.com
www.radiogifts.live
www.insightsdestinations.com
https://www.facebook.com/insightscounselingcenter/

DAY 181 – FOCUS

> "Your whole life is a manifestation of the thoughts that go on in your head." - Lisa Nichols

What you focus on grows. So, take a look at what you were focusing on just before you started reading this. Is it something you want to have more of in your life? If not, take a deep breath. Acknowledge the negative thought. Wrap it in a bubble, and watch it float away. Rinse and repeat.

_____

_____

_____

ABOUT THE AUTHOR

Karin Weiri, LMFT, Therapist, Break Through Life Coach, Speaker, Radio Talk Show Host
Orange City, Florida
Insights Counseling Center, Inc.
www.insightscounselingcenter.com
www.insightsblissfulretreats.com
www.radiogifts.live
www.insightsdestinations.com
https://www.facebook.com/insightscounselingcenter/

DAY 182 – BUILD A HAPPY BRAIN

> "There are only two ways to live your life. One is as though nothing is a miracle. The other is as though everything is a miracle." - Albert Einstein

We don't have control of very many things. We do have control over how we respond to life situations and what information we allow to enter our brains. We also have control over whom we spend time. Inundate yourself with positive, motivational, and uplifting information and people. Listen to podcasts that lift you up. This is necessary to help build new neuropathways in the brain that build a happy brain.

_____

_____

_____

ABOUT THE AUTHOR

Karin Weiri, LMFT, Therapist, Break Through Life Coach, Speaker, Radio Talk Show Host
Orange City, Florida
Insights Counseling Center, Inc.
www.insightscounselingcenter.com
www.insightsblissfulretreats.com
www.radiogifts.live
www.insightsdestinations.com
https://www.facebook.com/insightscounselingcenter/

DAY 183 – THE BIGGER THE SETBACK, THE BIGGER THE COMEBACK

"Sometimes what seems to be the worst thing that ever happened to you, turns out to be the best thing that ever happened to you." - Steve Jobs, 2005 Stanford Commencement Speech

When you feel as though you have hit bottom, emotionally, financially, spiritually – that is when you have the opportunity to do something that you otherwise would have been afraid to do, because there is nothing else to lose! So when things look like they are falling apart, you are actually getting into alignment with your purpose in life!

_____

_____

_____

ABOUT THE AUTHOR

Karin Weiri, LMFT, Therapist, Break Through Life Coach, Speaker, Radio Talk Show Host
Orange City, Florida
Insights Counseling Center, Inc.
www.insightscounselingcenter.com
www.insightsblissfulretreats.com
www.radiogifts.live
www.insightsdestinations.com
https://www.facebook.com/insightscounselingcenter/

DAY 184 – WHAT IS YOUR WHY?

"Stop saying what you can't do and set your mind to what is doable!" - Lanee Smith

Ask yourself: What is your why? It should be

something for which you have great passion and doing it is not tantamount to work so it is not a job. Once you figure out what your "why" is, write down your plan and take action! Stop recalibrate your focus to what is achievable rather than staying idle in the chasm of doubt.

Once you are living in your

passion, success will follow.

_____

_____

_____

ABOUT THE AUTHOR

Lanee Smith is a magazine publisher and author who writes to inspire, empower and encourage women to become successful.
bayareamag@gmail.com
fb.me/laneeonline

DAY 185 – ACCEPT WHAT WE CANNOT ALTER – PART 1

"Acceptance doesn't mean approval." - Unknown

Webster's Dictionary says "acceptance is the action of consenting to receive or undertake something offered". It means that you are consenting to the situation. People feel that if they accept a situation, that they agree with the situation. That is not true. We do not approve of the situation, we simply accept that it is what it is. Doing this allows us to look at the situation from a fresh and different perspective.

_____

_____

_____

ABOUT THE AUTHOR

Phillis Menschner, MSW LCSW
Maitland, Florida
menschnercounsel@aol.com
Facebook is menschnercounsel

DAY 186 – ACCEPT WHAT WE CANNOT ALTER – PART 2

"I am not going to walk in the path of complaint. I am going to walk in the path of acceptance." - Iyanla Vanzant

When we are dissatisfied or annoyed, we complain. We are frustrated that we cannot control something. Instead of complaining, try accepting the situation for what it is. Do not waste energy trying to control that which is not yours to control. A sense of freedom is then found within.

ABOUT THE AUTHOR

Phillis Menschner, MSW LCSW
Maitland, Florida
menschnercounsel@aol.com
Facebook is menschnercounsel

DAY 187 – HOW TO DEVELOP A WEALTHY MINDSET

"If you want to become Wealthy, you must first change your mindset. A wealthy mindset has nothing to do with how much money you make, but how you view yourself and the world around you. Accept the poor choices of your past and make a commitment to making wiser decisions for your future."- Cintia Pedone

Here are four steps you can start now:

1. Release all limiting beliefs about yourself, people, and the world around you.

2. Remove your thoughts of mediocrity and victimization.

3. See yourself with a positive mindset; love yourself.

4. Remember you can only control you. Self-reflect on every situation and interaction with the goal to better yourself.

It's now time to reprogram our mind and create a vision for your future. You deserve a healthy, wealthy, and happy life. You are in control.

_____

_____

_____

ABOUT THE AUTHOR

Cintia Pedone
FB & IG: Cintia Diamond Consulting
info@cintiadiamondconsulting.com
www.CintiaDiamondConsulting.com

DAY 188 – LEVERAGE YOUR WAY TO WEALTH: TOP 3 THINGS THE WEALTHY DO TO CREATE LEVERAGE

"It's time to get ahead. Leverage is one key component to building wealth faster." - Cintia Pedone

Three things the wealthy do to create leverage.

1. Insure your assets. We can't control what happens to us, but we can be financially protected when it does. Wealthy people leverage insurance companies to cover the financial burden associated with risk (illness, disability, divorce, and death) instead of using their own money or get into debt.

2. Have a sound financial plan.

3. Get incorporated and leverage the tax code.

_____

_____

_____

ABOUT THE AUTHOR

Cintia Pedone
FB & IG: Cintia Diamond Consulting
info@cintiadiamondconsulting.com
www.CintiaDiamondConsulting.com

DAY 189 — LEVERAGE YOUR WAY TO WEALTH - INSURE YOUR ASSETS

"The wealthy understand that they are the #1 asset, they insure themselves and their ability to earn income. You are the #1 Money Maker." - Cintia Pedone

Who is a necessary part of the wealth creation equation? You! So, what is the first step in any sound financial plan? Insurance. The proper insurance plans are essential to continued cashflow during unexpected life events such as a major illness, disability, divorce, law suits, and death. Passing on your wealth is done through proper insurance planning. Making sure you have the right plan is key to protecting any loss.

Visit www.yourguidetolifeinsurance.com for your complimentary guide to protect your assets!

_____

_____

_____

ABOUT THE AUTHOR

Cintia Pedone
FB & IG: Cintia Diamond Consulting
info@cintiadiamondconsulting.com
www.CintiaDiamondConsulting.com

DAY 190 – MUSTARD SEED FAITH

"Now faith is the substance of things hoped for, the evidence of things not seen" - Hebrews 11:1

I have reached the mountain top and touched the rainbows in my lifetime. But, in recent years, the opposite has been true. I found myself deeply depressed, immensely anxious, and unforgettably hopeless. But, God! He hid me in a dark and secret place, where He met my needs. I didn't think I would make it. Now, I can stand from the other side, because I never let go of my faith!

_____

_____

_____

ABOUT THE AUTHOR

Kim is COO/Co-owner of Carte Blanche Events, LLC an event planning and facilitation company and owner of Carte Blanche Travel.
Kimberly Purnell
Chicago, Illinois
www.carteblancheme2.com
info@carteblancheme2.com
www.facebook.com/carteblancheevents

DAY 191 — I AM MORE THAN A CONQUEROR!

"Above all, taking the shield of faith, wherewith ye shall be able to quench all the fiery darts of the wicked." - Ephesians 6:16

"It's back!" That was what my mom was told for the third time in her life. Breast cancer has struck, again! Why my mom, God? And His reply was: "Why not, your mom?" I began to see her transform into this woman of courage, strength, and tremendous faith as a result of her journey. Her test has become her testimony. She has touched so many women's lives by sharing her journey. I'm rejoicing in the truth that she is again, cancer free!

_____

_____

_____

ABOUT THE AUTHOR

Kim is COO/Co-owner of Carte Blanche Events, LLC an event planning and facilitation company and owner of Carte Blanche Travel.
Kimberly Purnell
Chicago, Illinois
www.carteblancheme2.com
info@carteblancheme2.com
www.facebook.com/carteblancheevents

DAY 192 – WHOM THE SON SETS FREE IS FREE INDEED

"It is for freedom that Christ has set us free. Stand firm, then, and do not let yourselves be burdened again by a yoke of slavery." - Galatians 5:1

"People pleaser!" How long will I live to please others? How long will I put the cares of others above my own? There is bondage associated with people-pleasing and now I am finding myself breaking free. I search myself for meaning, identify, and clarity daily. "I'm important too!" Stop putting yourself at the bottom of the list. Implement self-care strategies. Learn to love yourself and value the choices you make for yourself!

_____

_____

_____

ABOUT THE AUTHOR

Kim is COO/Co-owner of Carte Blanche Events, LLC an event planning and facilitation company and owner of Carte Blanche Travel.
Kimberly Purnell
Chicago, Illinois
www.carteblancheme2.com
info@carteblancheme2.com
www.facebook.com/carteblancheevents

DAY 193 – AM I MY SISTER'S KEEPER?

"For you were called to freedom, brothers. Only do not use your freedom as an opportunity for the flesh, but through love serve one another." - Galatians 5:13

I am four years older than my youngest sister. We have always been two peas in a pod. I am so proud to be her big sister. Last year when I fell ill, I couldn't take care of myself. My sister would drive over an hour to come to tend to me. She nursed me back to health. I am well and grateful! When we serve one another, we experience the hand of God and His freedom.

_____

_____

_____

ABOUT THE AUTHOR

Kim is COO/Co-owner of Carte Blanche Events, LLC an event planning and facilitation company and owner of Carte Blanche Travel.
Kimberly Purnell
Chicago, Illinois
www.carteblancheme2.com
info@carteblancheme2.com
www.facebook.com/carteblancheevents

DAY 194 – SHOW ME THE MONEY!

"Let no debt remain outstanding, except the continuing debt to love one another, for whoever loves others has fulfilled the law." - Romans 13:8

There was a time when I used to chase the dangling carrot of my career. I knew full well that I should have moved on. I kept getting offered more money and as a single parent, financial needs were always paramount. At the end of the day, I over-stayed my welcome and ultimately lost my job, after many years of service. My lesson was never to put money before what matters most: family.

_____

_____

_____

ABOUT THE AUTHOR

Kim is COO/Co-owner of Carte Blanche Events, LLC an event planning and facilitation company and owner of Carte Blanche Travel.
Kimberly Purnell
Chicago, Illinois
www.carteblancheme2.com
info@carteblancheme2.com
www.facebook.com/carteblancheevents

DAY 195 – FREELY YOU GIVE, FREELY YOU SHALL RECEIVE

"Give, and it will be given to you. Good measure, pressed down, shaken together, running over, will be put into your lap. For with the measure you use it will be measured back to you." - Luke 6:38

I was raised to tithe as a young girl. Over the years, I moved away from tithing faithfully. There was a major difference in what I was reaping. I began to experience lack and a feeling of desperation around money. No amount was ever enough. It took me awhile, but I ultimately realized that I was short-changing God. I was not faithful with little so, He could not trust me with more.

_____

_____

_____

ABOUT THE AUTHOR

Kim is COO/Co-owner of Carte Blanche Events, LLC an event planning and facilitation company and owner of Carte Blanche Travel.
Kimberly Purnell
Chicago, Illinois
www.carteblancheme2.com
info@carteblancheme2.com
www.facebook.com/carteblancheevents

DAY 196 – REFLECTION IN THE MIRROR

"To thine own self be true." - Shakespeare

Wearing a mask is prevalent in today's society. What is my public persona versus my true one? Why are they not the same? I had to begin doing the intentional work of self-analysis and discovery. It took time, however, today I trust myself, I love myself, and I believe in myself. I have freed myself from the expectations of others in the world. I cast all my fears and anxieties into the great abyss and live life, on purpose!

_____

_____

_____

ABOUT THE AUTHOR

Kim is COO/Co-owner of Carte Blanche Events, LLC an event planning and facilitation company and owner of Carte Blanche Travel.
Kimberly Purnell
Chicago, Illinois
www.carteblancheme2.com
info@carteblancheme2.com
www.facebook.com/carteblancheevents

DAY 197 – I SING BECAUSE I'M FREE

"The secret to happiness is freedom, the secret to freedom is courage." - Thucydides Quotes

"I sing because I'm happy. I sing because I'm free." This is a verse from one of my favorite songs, "His Eye is on the Sparrow." There is a freedom that comes with knowing that God is watching over me. I have become emboldened, confident, and courageous. No longer will I fear being judged or fear any failures. I am authentically me and I will walk in my purpose with fervor and grace.

_____

_____

_____

ABOUT THE AUTHOR

Kim is COO/Co-owner of Carte Blanche Events, LLC an event planning and facilitation company and owner of Carte Blanche Travel.
Kimberly Purnell
Chicago, Illinois
www.carteblancheme2.com
info@carteblancheme2.com
www.facebook.com/carteblancheevents

DAY 198 – FIND THE DIAMOND IN YOU!

"The fire of the diamond of true identity is always there; it just needs the Masters' crafting to reveal it." - Kenneth G. Mills

Diamonds begin as graphite, the same mineral in pencil lead. Diamonds undergo intense heat and pressure before it emerges as a strong, yet precious gem. With too much pressure, pencil lead is easily broken. Queens, life will take you through intense heat and pressure which can make you question your ability to withstand. Look within and you will find that everything you need you already have, because God put it there!

_____

_____

_____

ABOUT THE AUTHOR

Dr. Lya Redmond is a therapist and author. Her publishing company, Red Sun Publications, launches in 2019.
Lya Redmond, Ed.D.
Philadelphia, Pennsylvania
www.facebook.com/lya.ravenellredmond

DAY 199 – THE LIVING WATER

"You are a garden fountain, a well of flowing water streaming down from Lebanon." - Song of Songs 4:15

I am most passionate about empowering everyone around me. So, whether it is a book, advice or a pep talk, I like to share with others and give them what I call "Living Water." If we can pour encouragement and faith into others, this is the true healing that has been passed down to us. No matter what the pain is, you can't give up now.

_____

_____

_____

ABOUT THE AUTHOR

Erika was raised in Charleston, SC. She is a US Army Veteran and is a mother of one. She helps families find financial freedom and build generational wealth.
Erika Simmons
Senior Associate World Financial Group
Winter Park, Florida
https://www.wfgconnects.com/erikasimmons
www.instagram.com/1stladyerika
https://www.facebook.com/erikachesimmons

DAY 200 – CHARACTER LEADS TO PURPOSE

"A good name is more desirable than great riches; to be esteemed is better than silver or gold." – Proverbs 22:1

I love meeting people that understand the principle of leaving a legacy for their families. I align my with those who want more out of life, with a network of women and men of character and purpose. No matter what their paycheck is, people have a purpose. I work with leaders and leaders in the making. We all have something to learn from one another.

_____

_____

_____

ABOUT THE AUTHOR

Erika was raised in Charleston, SC. She is a US Army Veteran and is a mother of one. She helps families find financial freedom and build generational wealth.
Erika Simmons
Senior Associate World Financial Group
Winter Park, Florida
https://www.wfgconnects.com/erikasimmons
www.instagram.com/1stladyerika
https://www.facebook.com/erikachesimmons

DAY 201 – GIVE YOU A TRY

"It's ok to fail. If I fail, at least I know I tried to do something. If I don't try to do anything, nothing will ever happen." - Jay Anise

Giving up is easy. Do you know what's even easier? Not ever starting. My question is, "Do you want to live a complacent life of comfort or a challenging life of unstoppable purpose?" In order to live with purpose, you have to make a move. You never truly fail when you take a step, no matter how big or small. Don't let your mind get in the way. Give YOU a try!

_____

_____

_____

ABOUT THE AUTHOR

Jasmine "Jay Anise" Hendrix: Founder of *Never Outta Ink*, Best Selling Author, RN, Writer, Poet, Mother, and Servant of God.
Jay Anise
Birmingham, Alabama
www.neverouttaink.com
jayanise@neverouttaink.com
www.facebook.com/writerjayanise

DAY 202 – SAY YES TO YOU

"God is within her, she will not fall; God will help her at break of day." - Psalm 46:5 (NIV)

We easily place everyone else's needs above our own. We make excuses for why we do not have time for self-care. We reason that by adding ourselves into the equation, it will be too overwhelming. Well, that changes today! Your life does not work without you! Take a step back and refocus your mind. You will not fail with God on your side! God dwells within you, so you cannot be destroyed.

_____

_____

_____

ABOUT THE AUTHOR

Jasmine "Jay Anise" Hendrix: Founder of Never Outta Ink, Best Selling Author, RN, Writer, Poet, Mother, and Servant of God.
Jay Anise
Birmingham, Alabama
www.neverouttaink.com
jayanise@neverouttaink.com
www.facebook.com/writerjayanise

DAY 203 — NO COMPARISON

> "I am enough. To others, I do not compare. So stand with me now and boldly say, I KNOW WHO I AM!" - Jay Anise (Excerpt from "I AM")

God made you special. You don't have to be like anyone else in order to succeed. You aren't truly living when you compare your journey to another person's journey. God can't direct your path when you are on someone else's road. Your destiny is delayed when you are focused on someone else's process and not on the promises of God. You are enough just the way you are. What God has for you is for you!

_____

_____

_____

ABOUT THE AUTHOR

Jasmine "Jay Anise" Hendrix: Founder of Never Outta Ink, Best Selling Author, RN, Writer, Poet, Mother, and Servant of God.
Jay Anise
Birmingham, Alabama
www.neverouttaink.com
jayanise@neverouttaink.com
www.facebook.com/writerjayanise

DAY 204 — NEW DIRT

"I will not let anyone walk through my mind with their dirty feet." - Mahatma Gandhi

Who, in your life is tracking mud across your mind? Is it someone else or is it you? Yes, your feet can be just as dirty as others. Don't give anyone permission to control your thoughts or actions. You must rid yourself from whatever is adding mud in your life. Clean it up and not just the bare minimum by running your feet under water. Use soap to activate the cleansing process. Let the mud wash away for a start fresh. Tomorrow, there will be new dirt.

_____

_____

_____

ABOUT THE AUTHOR

Jasmine "Jay Anise" Hendrix: Founder of Never Outta Ink, Best Selling Author, RN, Writer, Poet, Mother, and Servant of God.
Jay Anise
Birmingham, Alabama
www.neverouttaink.com
jayanise@neverouttaink.com
www.facebook.com/writerjayanise

DAY 205 – THE POWER OF AFFIRMATIONS

"Death and life are in the power of the tongue: and they that love it shall eat the fruit thereof." - Proverbs 18:21 (KJV)

What are you speaking over your life? Every day, look into the mirror and speak positivity over yourself. I believe in you yet, I have not met you. You are beautiful. You are strong. You will not be defeated. You will achieve your dreams. You are no longer bound. You can do it. You are a child of God. Your business will flourish. You are overflowing with abundance.

_____

_____

_____

ABOUT THE AUTHOR

Jasmine "Jay Anise" Hendrix: Founder of Never Outta Ink, Best Selling Author, RN, Writer, Poet, Mother, and Servant of God.
Jay Anise
Birmingham, Alabama
www.neverouttaink.com
jayanise@neverouttaink.com
www.facebook.com/writerjayanise

DAY 206 – STARVE YOUR DISTRACTIONS

"Elevation requires you to starve your distractions and feed your enhancements." - JayAnise

Live a life so focused that everything has to take a back seat to who God has called you to be. Make your fears hungry. Make your doubts hungry. Starve your insecurities, your comparison issues, and your low self-esteem. Feed the parts of you that help you grow. Feed your spirit and your mind with positivity. Give your time and energy to things that elevate you beyond the mundane.

_____

_____

_____

ABOUT THE AUTHOR

Jasmine "Jay Anise" Hendrix: Founder of Never Outta Ink, Best Selling Author, RN, Writer, Poet, Mother, and Servant of God.
Jay Anise
Birmingham, Alabama
www.neverouttaink.com
jayanise@neverouttaink.com
www.facebook.com/writerjayanise

DAY 207 – THERE IS NO PRESENT WITHOUT YOUR PAST

"Life can only be understood backwards; but it must be lived forwards." – Soren Kierkegaard

How did I become a best-selling author? I realized what I was capable of achieving by accepting who God called me to be. I stopped hiding from the things that, at one time, broke me and began sharing my story. I didn't let the pain of my past stop me from reaching my purpose for today. You may not understand right now, but there is a reason for your struggle. You will come out stronger and one day it will all make sense.

_____

_____

_____

ABOUT THE AUTHOR

Jasmine "Jay Anise" Hendrix: Founder of Never Outta Ink, Best Selling Author, RN, Writer, Poet, Mother, and Servant of God.
Jay Anise
Birmingham, Alabama
www.neverouttaink.com
jayanise@neverouttaink.com
www.facebook.com/writerjayanise

DAY 208 – PUT IT ON PAPER

"A dream written down with a date becomes a goal. A goal broken down into steps becomes a plan. A plan backed by action makes your dreams come true."
- Greg Reid

It's time to get your dreams out of your head and put them on paper. Writing it down makes it real. You can become easily confused and overwhelmed when attempting to execute goals that are in your mind. Make a list of what you want to accomplish, how you plan to do it, and when you plan on taking the action steps required. Give yourself a deadline and write it down.

_____

_____

_____

ABOUT THE AUTHOR

Jasmine "Jay Anise" Hendrix: Founder of Never Outta Ink, Best Selling Author, RN, Writer, Poet, Mother, and Servant of God.
Jay Anise
Birmingham, Alabama
www.neverouttaink.com
jayanise@neverouttaink.com
www.facebook.com/writerjayanise

DAY 209 – LET US PRAY

> "Therefore I tell you, whatever you ask in prayer, believe that you have received it, and it will be yours." - Mark 11:24 (NIV)

"Father God the person who is reading this needs to hear your voice right now. I am asking that you cover them and supply their every need. Allow them to be still and focus on you and your word. Guide their steps and direct their paths. I am praying for clarity and peace over their minds and their decisions. I pray that they are bold in their walk and faith in you. In Jesus name I pray, Amen."

_____

_____

_____

ABOUT THE AUTHOR

Jasmine "Jay Anise" Hendrix: Founder of Never Outta Ink, Best Selling Author, RN, Writer, Poet, Mother, and Servant of God.
Jay Anise
Birmingham, Alabama
www.neverouttaink.com
jayanise@neverouttaink.com
www.facebook.com/writerjayanise

DAY 210 – LESS = MORE

"Listening, Engaging, Speaking, and Seeing yields More Freedom, More Success, and More Stability" - Jay Anise

The LESS acronym has helped me so much! When you need a little uplifting, apply these tools. Start your days by Listening to inspirational videos, podcasts, or music. Engage in positive conversations with your peers. Speak positive affirmations over your life. Write down three things that you love about yourself so you can See on paper how great you actually are. Apply this to your life now and watch how your mindset and your life begin to change.

_____

_____

_____

ABOUT THE AUTHOR

Jasmine "Jay Anise" Hendrix: Founder of Never Outta Ink, Best Selling Author, RN, Writer, Poet, Mother, and Servant of God.
Jay Anise
Birmingham, Alabama
www.neverouttaink.com
jayanise@neverouttaink.com
www.facebook.com/writerjayanise

DAY 211 – A POWERFUL WORD

"In the beginning was the Word, and the Word was with God, and the Word was God." - John 1:1 (KJV)

We experience a wide variety of emotions in our lives. We deal with heartache and breakthrough, health scares, midnight blues, financial increase and positive news. One day we can be on top of the world and the next we can be on the complete opposite side of the spectrum. One thing that never changes, and that will always see us through, is the Word of God. His word is everlasting.

_____

_____

_____

ABOUT THE AUTHOR

Jasmine "Jay Anise" Hendrix: Founder of Never Outta Ink, Best Selling Author, RN, Writer, Poet, Mother, and Servant of God.
Jay Anise
Birmingham, Alabama
www.neverouttaink.com
jayanise@neverouttaink.com
www.facebook.com/writerjayanise

DAY 212 – BE AGGRESSIVE

"Never stop fighting until you arrive at your destined place - that is, the unique you." - A. P. J. Abdul Kalam

Say, you put some money into a vending machine. You make your selection, but your item gets stuck. We tap or shake the machine to get the item. We use a little force if it does not fall. What if we did the same thing in our life? You have to be intentional and aggressive when it comes to yourself. Go after what you want. Go after what you deserve. Persevere. Shake the vending machine of life.

_____

_____

_____

ABOUT THE AUTHOR

Jasmine "Jay Anise" Hendrix: Founder of Never Outta Ink, Best Selling Author, RN, Writer, Poet, Mother, and Servant of God.
Jay Anise
Birmingham, Alabama
www.neverouttaink.com
jayanise@neverouttaink.com
www.facebook.com/writerjayanise

DAY 213 – ATTACK OR FALL BACK

"In every battle there comes a time when both sides consider themselves beaten, then he who continues the attack wins." - Ulysses S. Grant

You possess all of the tools that you need to be successful. Your destiny depends on what you bring to the surface. Load yourself with a positive mentality, faith, determination, and God. You may not have all of the answers or resources alone. God has already placed within you enough substance to win. Attack the enemy. Attack negativity when it comes into your mind. Otherwise, you might watch someone else carry your blessings.

_____

_____

_____

ABOUT THE AUTHOR

Jasmine "Jay Anise" Hendrix: Founder of Never Outta Ink, Best Selling Author, RN, Writer, Poet, Mother, and Servant of God.
Jay Anise
Birmingham, Alabama
www.neverouttaink.com
jayanise@neverouttaink.com
www.facebook.com/writerjayanise

DAY 214 – LOCK IN POSITIVE THOUGHTS

"No one can enter your mind without your permission when you hold the keys."
- JayAnise

You have the keys to your mind! So, the only way that the enemy or anyone else can invade your head space is if you hand control over. Do not allow that negativity to come and go as it pleases. Lock in what God says about you. He says that you are the light of the world. You are an incredible work of art. You were created in his likeness. Lock in positive thoughts and safeguard the keys.

_____

_____

_____

ABOUT THE AUTHOR

Jasmine "Jay Anise" Hendrix: Founder of Never Outta Ink, Best Selling Author, RN, Writer, Poet, Mother, and Servant of God.
Jay Anise
Birmingham, Alabama
www.neverouttaink.com
jayanise@neverouttaink.com
www.facebook.com/writerjayanise

DAY 215 – WHO IS IN YOUR CIRCLE?

"As iron sharpens iron, so one person sharpens another." - Proverbs 27:17 (NIV)

At times, we do not let people in because we have a superwoman mentality telling us that we do not need anyone. Sometimes we have been hurt by someone in the past. Do not let either reason keep you from connecting with people. I have learned that building community is a large part of growth, both personally and in business. Surround yourself with like-minded people that can help hold you accountable. We are stronger together.

_____

_____

_____

ABOUT THE AUTHOR

Jasmine "Jay Anise" Hendrix: Founder of Never Outta Ink, Best Selling Author, RN, Writer, Poet, Mother, and Servant of God.
Jay Anise
Birmingham, Alabama
www.neverouttaink.com
jayanise@neverouttaink.com
www.facebook.com/writerjayanise

DAY 216 — NEGATIVE THOUGHT, POSITIVE TALK

"I believe that words are strong, that they can overwhelm what we fear when fear seems more awful than life is good." - Andrew Solomon

Since we know that negative thoughts will be present most times during our trials and hardships, then we have to be ready with a quick response. If you think "I'm broke.", then speak "I am walking into financial increase.". If you think "I'll never receive that type of love," then speak, "The Lord will bless me with someone who will love me genuinely and unconditionally." These responses seems like a minor task, but the results are major. #NegativeThoughtPositiveTalk

_____

_____

_____

ABOUT THE AUTHOR

Jasmine "Jay Anise" Hendrix: Founder of Never Outta Ink, Best Selling Author, RN, Writer, Poet, Mother, and Servant of God.
Jay Anise
Birmingham, Alabama
www.neverouttaink.com
jayanise@neverouttaink.com
www.facebook.com/writerjayanise

DAY 217 — WHERE IS YOUR FOCUS?

"Ye are of God, little children, and have overcome them: because greater is he that is in you, than he that is in the world." - I John 4:4 KJV

Right now, God is saying, "Can you focus on me.?" Stop worrying about what everyone else is doing. Stop catching up on the latest episodes of your favorite television show. Stop scrolling social media during every free moment that you have. In order to bless you with what He has already planned for your life, God needs your undivided attention. Everything else can wait. Where you place your focus will determine the type of life you live.

_____

_____

_____

ABOUT THE AUTHOR

Jasmine "Jay Anise" Hendrix: Founder of Never Outta Ink, Best Selling Author, RN, Writer, Poet, Mother, and Servant of God.
Jay Anise
Birmingham, Alabama
www.neverouttaink.com
jayanise@neverouttaink.com
www.facebook.com/writerjayanise

DAY 218 — GET MONEY, KEEP MONEY

"A budget is telling your money where to go instead of wondering where it went."
- Dave Ramsey

So there is no magic trick to help you save money. There is one word that I have found to be extremely beneficial and that is budget. I worked the same job with the same bills for 2 years. The first year, I lived paycheck to paycheck. The second year, after budgeting, I began to save money every payday. When you list where your money is going, you save yourself from spending unnecessarily. Give it a try.

_____

_____

_____

ABOUT THE AUTHOR

Jasmine "Jay Anise" Hendrix: Founder of Never Outta Ink, Best Selling Author, RN, Writer, Poet, Mother, and Servant of God.
Jay Anise
Birmingham, Alabama
www.neverouttaink.com
jayanise@neverouttaink.com
www.facebook.com/writerjayanise

DAY 219 – THE PRAYER OF JABEZ PART 1

"Jabez cried out to the God of Israel, "Oh, that you would bless me and enlarge my territory! Let your hand be with me, and keep me from harm so that I will be free from pain." And God granted his request." – 1 Chronicles 4:10

This scripture is the only time that Jabez is mentioned in the bible. Such a little request that Jabez, and just like that, God granted his request. I think sometimes in Business, we often think that success comes with longevity. Just what if, it's all in the power of your simple request to God. "Bless me and enlarge my territory", and his request was granted. So, what if? Just send your request to God and believe He will answer it.

_____

_____

_____

ABOUT THE AUTHOR

Life Coach with compassion for community which is the driving force of my non-profit, UMAD, United Mothers and Daughters.
Erica Hicks
Mserica.Hicks@Yahoo.com
Facebook-erica.hicks.980
www.shapedlikeagoddess.com

DAY 220 – THE PRAYER OF JABEZ PART 2

"Jabez cried out to the God of Israel, "Oh, that you would bless me and enlarge my territory! Let your hand be with me, and keep me from harm so that I will be free from pain." And God granted his request." – 1 Chronicles 4:10

The moment I started praying that prayer, I saw little miracles start to happen. When I say little, I mean the things we often ignore, like a new connection, a new friend on Facebook. An opportunity to leave your business card in a restaurant. A discount at the office supply store, where you get your home office supplies. God will grant your request, just go before him and tell him what you need.

_____

_____

_____

ABOUT THE AUTHOR

Life Coach with compassion for community which is the driving force of my non-profit, UMAD, United Mothers and Daughters.
Erica Hicks
Mserica.Hicks@Yahoo.com
Facebook-erica.hicks.980
www.shapedlikeagoddess.com

DAY 221 – LIVE FREE OF THE THOUGHTS AND EMOTIONS WEIGHING YOU DOWN

"Emancipate yourselves from mental slavery; none but ourselves can free our minds." - Bob Marley

Are you living with uncertain mental and emotional instability? Do you feel stressed, overworked, spent, and alone? Does it feel like your thoughts and emotions are constantly weighing you down and controlling your dreams and goals?

Begin noticing your beliefs and thoughts patterns to understand how to take on the stress, anxiety, regrets, shame, fears, self-doubts, and past sufferings that are weighing you down. Create clarity and confidence to take on any challenge. Retrain new neuropathways that will lead you to accomplish any goal you want to achieve.

_____

_____

_____

ABOUT THE AUTHOR

Tammy helps children and adults create the mind, body, & spirit they desire with HypnoCoaching & Wellness programs.
Tammy Workman-Lopez
ATouchThatGivesBack.com
TammyWorkman@ATouchThatGivesBack.com

DAY 222 – TIME TO FIND YOUR HOPE

"Before I learned to stop my mind, I thought of death a lot. Now I think and live into my passion" - Tony S

Have you lost hope? Have you done everything to fix the challenges in your life and yet just feel heavier? You are not alone and you don't have to stay there. You have some beliefs that have created self-sabotaging habits on the subconscious level. Check your thinking, allow support to help you shift and refocus, and you will create freedom, abundance, confidence and healthy boundaries.

_____

_____

_____

ABOUT THE AUTHOR

Tammy helps children and adults create the mind, body, & spirit they desire with HypnoCoaching & Wellness programs.
Tammy Workman-Lopez
ATouchThatGivesBack.com
TammyWorkman@ATouchThatGivesBack.com

DAY 223 – BOUNCING BACK AFTER A MAJOR SETBACK

"For I know the plans I have for you," declares the Lord, "plans to prosper you and not to harm you, plans to give you hope and a future. - Jeremiah 29:11 (NIV)

If you have never encountered a major setback in life, count your blessings. Life happens to us all no matter what. It can be a stressful and overwhelming, especially if you are without a strong support system. Lean on your faith knowing that God makes no mistakes. If He brought you to it, He will bring you through it.

_____

_____

_____

ABOUT THE AUTHOR

Tabatha Spurlock, EdD is a wife, mother, educator, coach, entrepreneur, philanthropist, and leader in the community.
Dr. Tabatha M. W. Spurlock
Henrico, Virginia
www.empower1inspiremany.com
empower1inspiremany@gmail.com
www.facebook.com/empower1inspiremany

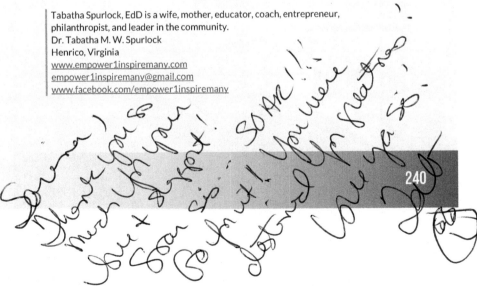

DAY 224 – EMPOWER ONE, INSPIRE MANY

"A man's gift maketh room for him, and bringeth him before great men." - Proverbs 18:16 (KJV)

In 2005, I became an education "career-switcher." It was one of the best decisions of my life. I quickly learned that educating and mentoring teenagers was challenging. While I wanted to save all of my disadvantaged students, I knew that was impossible. Instead, every day I decided to empower one and inspire many. Today, I am proud to have many former students who beat the odds and are successful adults.

_____

_____

_____

ABOUT THE AUTHOR

Tabatha Spurlock, EdD is a wife, mother, educator, coach, entrepreneur, philanthropist, and leader in the community.
Dr. Tabatha M. W. Spurlock
Henrico, Virginia
www.empower1inspiremany.com
empower1inspiremany@gmail.com
www.facebook.com/empower1inspiremany

DAY 225 — I EARNED THIS SEAT

"She is clothed with dignity and strength and she laughs without fear of the future." - Proverbs 31:25 (NLT)

What does it feel like to be the only woman and minority with a "seat at the table?" From my experiences, it is quite rewarding. There is no room for fear because the real battle has not yet happened! If no one listens when you speak while you are in the room, the seat becomes irrelevant. Hold your own and when opportunity knocks, be a spark of life for a fellow woman or person in the minority.

_____

_____

_____

ABOUT THE AUTHOR

Tabatha Spurlock, EdD is a wife, mother, educator, coach, entrepreneur, philanthropist, and leader in the community.
Dr. Tabatha M. W. Spurlock
Henrico, Virginia
www.empower1inspiremany.com
empower1inspiremany@gmail.com
www.facebook.com/empower1inspiremany

DAY 226 – IT'S OK TO JUMP

"I praise you because I'm fearfully and wonderfully made; your works are wonderful, I know that full well." - Psalm 139:14 (NIV)

Have you ever felt like you were giving 100% or more to a job or relationship only to feel unwanted or devalued? Why did you stay? Were you afraid or even fearful? If you answered yes, the next time, go to God. He will give you the discernment needed and confirm when it is time to jump. You are who He says you are and do not let anyone convince you otherwise.

_____

_____

_____

ABOUT THE AUTHOR

Tabatha Spurlock, EdD is a wife, mother, educator, coach, entrepreneur, philanthropist, and leader in the community.
Dr. Tabatha M. W. Spurlock
Henrico, Virginia
www.empower1inspiremany.com
empower1inspiremany@gmail.com
www.facebook.com/empower1inspiremany

DAY 227 – ROYALTY

"Think like a Queen. A Queen is not afraid to fall. Failure is another stone to greatness." - Oprah Winfrey

Crowns may shift but never fall. And we are fearless and wonderfully made. Understand, that the trials of life are prerequisites to your personal success. So, hold your head high, Queen. Reposition your crown and strut. Success is inevitable.

_____

_____

_____

ABOUT THE AUTHOR

Kimberly is a children's author, entrepreneur, child welfare consultant and advocate for youth in care within the juvenile justice system.
Kimberly McMillian
Chicago, Illinois
https://www.facebook.com/AuthorKimMcMillian/
https://www.amazon.com/New-School-Blues-Kimberly-McMillian/dp/

DAY 228 – ME FIRST

"We need to do a better job of putting ourselves higher on our own to do list." - First Lady Michelle Obama

We are the nurturers of the world. We are the fixers. We are situation unifiers and stress relievers. We do all of this while forgetting to turn the "we" into "me." When we take into account ourselves, it does not mean that we are careless; it means we are care - full.

Ladies release, recharge and refuel your to do list.

_____

_____

_____

ABOUT THE AUTHOR

Kimberly McMillian
Chicago, Illinois
https://www.facebook.com/AuthorKimMcMillian/
https://www.amazon.com/New-School-Blues-Kimberly-McMillian/dp/

DAY 229 – THE ESSENCE OF MONEY

"Love is like money... hard to find easy to lose." - Ally Mbululo

Money is just money and has no definite use until it has a meaning in your life. Statistics prove that a high percentage of lottery winners end up broke or worse off. It is because they are unprepared to manage the unexpected financial increase. Also, that money did not have significant meaning to them. What does money mean to you? What is your financial plan? Are you ready for financial abundance?

_____

_____

_____

ABOUT THE AUTHOR

Pamela Mantey
Www.ittakesmoneyhoney.com
https://www.facebook.com/ittakesmoneyhoneymagazine/
https://www.facebook.com/ittakesmoneyhoney/
Pamela@ittakesmoneyhoney.com

DAY 230 – STRATEGY FOR FINANCIAL FREEDOM

"The key to wealth <u>and</u> happiness in today's world is to create multiple streams of income using diverse business models and combinations of passive and active income in areas where your passions and talents can be most thoroughly engaged." - Jimmy DeMesa, MD, MBA

Everyone desires financial freedom, but not all will attain it. You do not get wealthy by saving. You do not get wealthy by eliminating debt either. You have to focus on one thing: creating cashflow. Engage in streams of income that create cashflow. That is how you will eliminate debt and have more savings. If you are a mom like me, you would like to work a few hours from home and earn more money.

_____

_____

_____

ABOUT THE AUTHOR

Pamela Mantey
Www.ittakesmoneyhoney.com
https://www.facebook.com/ittakesmoneyhoneymagazine/
https://www.facebook.com/ittakesmoneyhoney/
Pamela@ittakesmoneyhoney.com

DAY 231 – MONEY HAS POWER

"It's a kind of spiritual snobbery that makes people think they can be happy without money." - Albert Camus

The bottom line is that money has power to set you free or enslave you. It enslaves you by keeping you in unhealthy relationships, at a job you hate, dependent on the government as to when you can feed your family. Money enslaves and keeps you at a substandard lifestyle, living paycheck to paycheck. You cannot live the life you really desire to live when you are enslaved to money. It is time to be set free monetarily.

_____

_____

_____

ABOUT THE AUTHOR

Pamela Mantey
Www.ittakesmoneyhoney.com
https://www.facebook.com/ittakesmoneyhoneymagazine/
https://www.facebook.com/ittakesmoneyhoney/
Pamela@ittakesmoneyhoney.com

DAY 232 – CLUES TO YOUR REAL VALUES

"Don't tell me what you value, show me your budget, and I'll tell you what you value." - Joe Biden

What do you really value? Get a journal and document every penny you spend every day for a thirty days. Start on the first of the month or even today. At the end of each day, log into your online banking mobile app or have a look at your spending receipts. Write down every purchase you made. At the end of the thirty days, review it and write down how much you spent on different things. You should get a clear picture of where your values are. If you do not like it, change your spending habits to align with your values.

_____

_____

_____

ABOUT THE AUTHOR

Pamela Mantey
Www.ittakesmoneyhoney.com
https://www.facebook.com/ittakesmoneyhoneymagazine/
https://www.facebook.com/ittakesmoneyhoney/
Pamela@ittakesmoneyhoney.com

DAY 233 – A WOMAN CANNOT BE TRULY FREE UNTIL SHE IS FINANCIALLY FREE

"A feast is made for laughter, and wine maketh merry: but money answereth all things" - Ecclesiastes 10:29

When a woman takes charge of her money, she takes charge of her life. She does not make excuses when she does not have any. She takes responsibility for the decisions and choices that have led to her current financial level. She realizes that she needs money to fulfill her purpose and dreams much easier to manifest much smoother. When she knows this about money, she is not limited. She knows the value of investing in her future.

_____

_____

_____

ABOUT THE AUTHOR

Pamela Mantey
Www.ittakesmoneyhoney.com
https://www.facebook.com/ittakesmoneyhoneymagazine/
https://www.facebook.com/ittakesmoneyhoney/
Pamela@ittakesmoneyhoney.com

DAY 234 – BECOME A MONEY MAGNET

"Money is like a river. It flows where the conditions are conducive to its flow." - Jacintha Mpalyenkana.

It is important to have a healthy mindset and attitude about money. To have a good relationship with money. You can work hard but drive money away with negative subconscious money mindset. Mindsets like "money is evil," "rich people are mean," and "money is hard to accumulate." Your mindset and affirmation should be, 'I am a money maker. I make money easily and effortlessly. I am in control of money, it no longer controls me.'

_____

_____

_____

ABOUT THE AUTHOR

Pamela Mantey
Www.ittakesmoneyhoney.com
https://www.facebook.com/ittakesmoneyhoneymagazine/
https://www.facebook.com/ittakesmoneyhoney/
Pamela@ittakesmoneyhoney.com

DAY 235 – CHOICE AND CHANCE

"It is our choices what show what we truly are, far more than our abilities"- J.K. Rowling

As a child, we believed who our family is or what our family does, will define us. Financially unstable, working minimum wage jobs, toxic relationships, substance abuse - it will be our lives one day. This is simply not true. I broke the cycle of poverty and you can too! Small choices made with great intention can lead you out of the darkness.

_____

_____

_____

ABOUT THE AUTHOR

Alisha Rojas Harrison
Milford, Massachusetts
my.tupperware.com/alishaharrison
www.facebook.com/alisha.r.harrison
www.facebook.com/turtletupperware

DAY 236 – YOUR ENERGY: IS IT SERVING YOU OR DEPLETING YOU? PART 1

"Don't copy the behavior and customs of this world, but let God transform you into a new person by the way you think." - Romans 12:2NLT

As women, we are designed to have multiple roles and we are built with the capacity to serve gracefully within them. However, most of us were never taught how to serve. So instead of living and leading life, we find ourselves trying to balance our energy by multi-tasking and "doing life" in a way that never seems to serve our true heart's desires. Yet, we keep smiling and doing because if not us, then who?

_____

_____

_____

ABOUT THE AUTHOR

Dr. White is an Impact Coach whose story and proven systems serve as a valuable resource guide for high-performing entrepreneurs.
www.MineshaWhite.com
Facebook & IG: @DrMineshaWhite

DAY 237 — YOUR ENERGY: IS IT SERVING YOU OR DEPLETING YOU? PART 2

'Freedom is the will to be responsible to ourselves." - Friedrich Nietzsche

You are the glue that seems to hold everything and everyone together, so you are going to need something more sophisticated than a Google calendar to set your boundaries and support your efforts. Rethink where you are and regain your focus. You can serve from your rightful place of abundance. Receive more peace, joy, and fulfillment to living out your best life. Walk in freedom with peace, purpose and impact!

_____

_____

_____

ABOUT THE AUTHOR

Dr. White is an Impact Coach whose story and proven systems serve as a valuable resource guide for high-performing entrepreneurs.
www.MineshaWhite.com
Facebook & IG: @DrMineshaWhite

DAY 238 – A SEED OF FAITH

"Truly I tell you, if you have faith as small as a mustard seed, you can say to this mountain, 'Move from here to there,' and it will move. Nothing will be impossible for you." - Matthew 17:20

I made it to our last meeting when my adviser told me not to apply to Johns Hopkins or Yale Medical School. Accepted to both, I chose and graduated from Yale.

Years later, I fully understood his attempt to keep me in my place, so he could stay in his. Doors which seem closed can be opened, by faith. I will ever be grateful for that seed of faith in myself (planted by my mom). It has borne fruit over and again.

_____

_____

_____

ABOUT THE AUTHOR

Odett Stanley-Brown is Jamaican born, and married with four children. She has been a pediatrician for more than 30 years, last 18 in Central Florida. She loves God and loves life.
Odett Stanley-Brown, MD
Lady Lake, Florida
Nemours Health Systems

DAY 239 – COMMAND AND CREATE

"Unsuccessful people make decisions based on their current situations. Successful people make decisions based on where they want to be." - Unknown

Faith is a supernatural gift that we genetically inherit as believers. The level of faith that you obtain enables you to get a sneak peek into your future of what is to come.

Once faith is activated by your voice, it will command and create what you desire and what you need. Faith can take you where you belong and give you what is rightfully yours.

_____

_____

_____

ABOUT THE AUTHOR

Director of Kingdom Minded Women's Ministry, mandated to help women find their purpose and place in the kingdom.
Pastor Stephanie L. Hutton
Chicago, Illinois
www.kmwministry.com
https://www.facebook.com/kingdommindedwomen
@pastorstephhutton

DAY 240 — HOW BAD DO YOU WANT IT?

> "Some people succeed because they are destined but most because they are determined." - Unknown

Faith has the power to breakdown your walls of fears. Giving you the courage to go after not what you want, but what you desperately need. Leave your fears in the past. It has no place in your present, or in your future. Go after what you know is yours.

_____

_____

_____

ABOUT THE AUTHOR

Director of Kingdom Minded Women's Ministry, mandated to help women find their purpose and place in the kingdom.
Pastor Stephanie L. Hutton
Chicago, Illinois
www.kmwministry.com
https://www.facebook.com/kingdommindedwomen
@pastorstephhutton

DAY 241 – A SISTERS STRENGTH

"It's not the load that breaks you down, it's the way you carry it." - Lena Horne

Sisters, stay on the path headed for your heart's desires. When in darkness, shine your light bright.

When you feel you cannot run any longer, it's ok to skip.

When people speak negativity, let it fall on deaf ears.

When the load gets too heavy, carry it piece by piece.

What's most important is that you continue to move forward and you will soon get to that desired place.

_____

_____

_____

ABOUT THE AUTHOR

Kim is a teacher and event planner, mentor and empowers young minds, she is currently gearing up to launch a children's clothing line.
Kim Edwards-Hatch
Las Vegas, Nevada
hatchkim_teacher@yahoo.com
www.facebook.com/kim.edwardshatch

DAY 242 — EMBRACING YOUR GREATNESS

"A crown, if it hurts us, It's not worth wearing." - Pearl Bailey

Live your best life.

STOP walking in the shadows of doubt, fear and low self-esteem. STOP taking the back seat when you deserve to be the driver.

START being the greatness God created you to be. START by holding your head up and walking proudly.

Wear your tiara, my queen. If you don't own your greatness how can others?

_____

_____

_____

ABOUT THE AUTHOR

Kim is a teacher and event planner, mentor and empowers young minds, she is currently gearing up to launch a children's clothing line.
Kim Edwards-Hatch
Las Vegas, Nevada
hatchkim_teacher@yahoo.com
www.facebook.com/kim.edwardshatch

DAY 243 – ALWAYS BE A LIGHT

"You are the light of the world. …Let your light shine before others, so that they may see your good works and give glory to your Father who is in heaven." - Matthew 5:14-16

What energy are your bringing to the atmosphere? Life happens, and we must understand that it is necessary. Your response to unfortunate events will set the stage for what is to come. Always be a light, even in the darkest of times. Keep your flame lit and never lose faith. When triumph reaches your door, rejoice and humbly share it with the world. Show others that hard times will come, but they won't last always.

_____

_____

_____

ABOUT THE AUTHOR

Kristen "Minovét" Childs
Owner of Minovét - traveling boutique ~ Founder of Build-A-Boss Movement.
"Through health/financial struggles, I am still a light."
www.minovet.com
info@minovet.com
Facebook/Instagram/Twitter @SimplyMinovet
Facebook.com/groups/buildabossmovement

DAY 244 – LIGHT, LEAD THE WAY

"Darkness cannot drive out darkness; only light can do that. Hate cannot drive out hate; only love can do that." - Martin Luther King, Jr.

You have the ability to set the tone for your life. Be an inspiration to all, even the people that are watching and waiting for you to fail. The naysayers are also inspired by your success. Never stoop, belittle, or give petty reaction to those that doubt you. Show them that positivity and faith will take them a long way, regardless of their situation. Always be a light, and the light in others will always seek you out.

_____

_____

_____

ABOUT THE AUTHOR

Kristen "Minovét" Childs
Owner of Minovét - traveling boutique ~ Founder of Build-A-Boss Movement.
"Through health/financial struggles, I am still a light."
www.minovet.com
info@minovet.com
Facebook/Instagram/Twitter @SimplyMinovet
Facebook.com/groups/buildabossmovement

DAY 245 – FROM ORDINARY TO EXTRAORDINARY

> "I have a lot of things to prove to myself. One, is that I can live my life fearlessly."
> - Oprah Winfrey

If you are not learning, you are not growing and challenging yourself. True freedom lies in your ability to move from ordinary to extraordinary, even when the road seems scary. The power to live abundantly lies in your skills and abilities. Write down those areas in life in which you need to learn, grow and lead fearlessly. What do you need to do to live more fearlessly?

_____

_____

_____

ABOUT THE AUTHOR

Tywauna Wilson
Top Forty Under 40 | Leadership Maven | Personal Growth Coach | Clinical Laboratory Trailblazer | Best-Selling Author
Cincinnati, Ohio
www.coachteewilson.com
mailto:info@trendyelitellc.com
www.facebook.com/CoachTeeWilson
Instagram & Twitter: @Coachteewilson

DAY 246 – FAITH, YOUR SUPER POWER

"Faith is the first factor in a life devoted to service. Without it, nothing is possible. With it, nothing is impossible."- Mary McLeod Bethune

You achieve what you believe. Mustard seed faith is the super power needed to overcome your self-limiting beliefs. They come to cripple, steal, and destroy your dreams. When you begin to surrender your own understanding is when you start to achieve all that you are destined to become. That is when the real magic happens! In what areas of your life do you need more faith?

_____

_____

_____

ABOUT THE AUTHOR

Tywauna Wilson
Top Forty Under 40 | Leadership Maven | Personal Growth Coach | Clinical Laboratory Trailblazer | Best-Selling Author
Cincinnati, Ohio
www.coachteewilson.com
mailto:info@trendyelitellc.com
www.facebook.com/CoachTeeWilson
Instagram & Twitter: @Coachteewilson

DAY 247 – GIRL, YOU'RE WORTH IT!

> "Invest three percent of your income in yourself (self-development) in order to guarantee your future". - Brian Tracy

I remember asking an employer to pay for me to attend a conference and they told me no. I knew my attendance at the conference was critical to my life's plan, but I questioned if it was worth it for me to pay the cost. In hindsight, I was questioning if I was worth the investment. Have you ever missed out on an opportunity because you were afraid of the investment? What did it cost you?

_____

_____

_____

ABOUT THE AUTHOR

Tywauna Wilson
Top Forty Under 40 | Leadership Maven | Personal Growth Coach | Clinical Laboratory Trailblazer | Best-Selling Author
Cincinnati, Ohio
www.coachteewilson.com
mailto:info@trendyelitellc.com
www.facebook.com/CoachTeeWilson
Instagram & Twitter: @Coachteewilson

DAY 248 – DON'T EVEN TRIP, GOD HAS YOUR BACK!

"Do not be anxious about anything, but in every situation, by prayer and petition, with thanksgiving present your requests to God." - Philippians 4:6

When you think your back is up against the wall and you can hardly breathe that's when you know you are on the verge of your break through. It takes courage, determination, and grit to walk into your purpose. Yes, it is going to be scary, and you may have some fear. But with God, you will overcome and be blessed abundantly. Today, I challenge you to write your faith declaration and purpose.

_____

_____

_____

ABOUT THE AUTHOR

Tywauna Wilson
Top Forty Under 40 | Leadership Maven | Personal Growth Coach | Clinical Laboratory Trailblazer | Best-Selling Author
Cincinnati, Ohio
www.coachteewilson.com
mailto:info@trendyelitellc.com
www.facebook.com/CoachTeeWilson
Instagram & Twitter: @Coachteewilson

DAY 249 – THE POWER OF SELF PERCEPTION

"The way you perceive yourself is what you bring to yourself, so keep it positive!"- Dr. Kelly Bullock Daugherty

There are times when we allow negativity to overcome us. It weakens us and sometimes begins to diminish our self- worth. We feel like we can't help it and, we just aren't good enough. It is important to remember, during these times, that *positivity begets positivity.* Change your thinking. Change your approach. Maintain confidence in who you are and what you are capable of; and others will, too.

_____

_____

_____

ABOUT THE AUTHOR

Dr. Kelly Bullock Daugherty is an educator, national trainer, and CEO/Founder of Transitions Educational Consulting, LLC, Cleveland, Ohio
www.drkellybdaugherty.com
www.facebook.com/TransitionsEdConsult
Twitter: @DrKBDaugherty
TransitionsEducationalConsult@gmail.com

DAY 250 — GIFTED AND AMAZING

> "If you're always trying to be normal, you'll never know how AMAZING you can be!" - Maya Angelou

There is no question about it, you are absolutely amazing! You are intentionally and uniquely designed. You have a gift inside you. It is how you choose to nurture your gift that makes you extraordinary! Take a chance on yourself, step outside of what you normally do, and do not limit yourself to commonalities. Do not do what others expect. Do what stands out beyond the rest!

_____

_____

_____

ABOUT THE AUTHOR

Dr. Kelly Bullock Daugherty is an educator, national trainer, and CEO/Founder of Transitions Educational Consulting, LLC, Cleveland, Ohio
www.drkellybdaugherty.com
www.facebook.com/TransitionsEdConsult
Twitter: @DrKBDaugherty
TransitionsEducationalConsult@gmail.com

DAY 251 – NO LIMITS

"Life has no limitations except the ones you make." - Les Brown

The mind has the uncanny ability to make us believe we are unable to accomplish goals. Encountering these thoughts hindered me from taking risks for fear of failure. I learned that I had created these limitations for myself. The truth is, limitations are set in your own mind. You should know there are *no* limits to your greatness so do not waste time convincing yourself that you are anything less.

_____

_____

_____

ABOUT THE AUTHOR

Dr. Kelly Bullock Daugherty is an educator, national trainer, and CEO/Founder of Transitions Educational Consulting, LLC, Cleveland, Ohio
www.drkellybdaugherty.com
www.facebook.com/TransitionsEdConsult
Twitter: @DrKBDaugherty
TransitionsEducationalConsult@gmail.com

DAY 252 – PASSION & PURPOSE

"The purposes of a person's heart are deep waters, but one who has insight draws them out" - Proverbs 20:5 (NIV)

Throughout many phases of my life, I have come face to face with the question, "What is my purpose in life? Why am I here?" I have spent years contemplating exactly where I belong in this world. The fact is your purpose is fueled by your passion. Your passion is fueled by God. He is what connects your passion to your purpose. Follow His lead. Your passion and purpose will become clear.

_____

_____

_____

ABOUT THE AUTHOR

Dr. Kelly Bullock Daugherty is an educator, national trainer, and CEO/Founder of Transitions Educational Consulting, LLC, Cleveland, Ohio
www.drkellybdaugherty.com
www.facebook.com/TransitionsEdConsult
Twitter: @DrKBDaugherty
TransitionsEducationalConsult@gmail.com

DAY 253 – DON'T STOP

"Obstacles are detours in the right direction." - Gabby Bernstein

Obstacles are a natural part of life. They are often seen as negative since they tend to bring about frustration and other challenges. Obstacles should be seen as opportunities. They are opportunities for redirection; the chance to choose a different path toward your goal. The next time you are faced with an obstacle, call it a blessing. Face your new direction fearlessly. Whatever you do, don't stop!

_____

_____

_____

ABOUT THE AUTHOR

Dr. Kelly Bullock Daugherty is an educator, national trainer, and CEO/Founder of Transitions Educational Consulting, LLC, Cleveland, Ohio
www.drkellybdaugherty.com
www.facebook.com/TransitionsEdConsult
Twitter: @DrKBDaugherty
TransitionsEducationalConsult@gmail.com

DAY 254 – FAITH OVER FEAR

"For I know the plans I have for you, plans to prosper you and not harm you, plans to give you hope and a future." - Jeremiah 29:11

I have chosen to step out on faith, to walk into my destiny and fulfill what God intended for me and my family. After two marriages, three children and one grandchild, I finally can hear Gods voice clearer than ever before. I motivate people in business and look to inspire and help women step out on faith. Now, I help people walk into their destiny that was designed just for them.

_____

_____

_____

ABOUT THE AUTHOR

Shelley Johnson, Owner/Operator
Princess Anne, Maryland
Facebook Profile: Shelley Strawberri Johnson
Fiji 4 the kids Learning Center
www.fiji4thekids.net

DAY 255 – ON A DIVINE MISSION

> "He said to them, "Go into all the world and preach the gospel to all creation." - Mark 16:15

Walking in the purpose of God is my main mission. When God gave me the vision of helping women with a divine purpose, He showed me that this mission would not be easy. It was going to require much faith. My mission is to bless other women by educating, empowering, and equipping them with the knowledge they may need to become successful. I make myself available to those in need.

_____

_____

_____

ABOUT THE AUTHOR

Shelley Johnson, Owner/Operator
Princess Anne, Maryland
Facebook Profile: Shelley Strawberri Johnson
Fiji 4 the kids Learning Center
www.fiji4thekids.net

DAY 256 – IT'S TIME TO BOSS UP

Do you see a man skilled in his work? He will be stationed in the presence of kings; he will not stand before obscure men." - Proverbs 22:29

People who come together to network can share and empower one another on their goods and services. I'm a strong believer that, people are not looking for you they are looking for what you possess. I empower people to BOSS UP and manifest themselves. A lot of people live on the earth and never manifest themselves.

_____

_____

_____

ABOUT THE AUTHOR

Shelley Johnson, Owner/Operator
Princess Anne, Maryland
Facebook Profile: Shelley Strawberri Johnson
Fiji 4 the kids Learning Center
www.fiji4thekids.net

DAY 257 – STRENGTH

"I can do all things through Christ which strengtheneth me." - Philippians 4:13 (KJV)

In August 2018, my 18-year-old daughter, a college freshman, had a stroke. God kept my family and me through that major situation. We all face challenges in our lives. These obstacles make us who we are today. Each stumbling block is a building block, strengthening and building us up. This is what I know for sure, through personal experiences.

_____

_____

_____

ABOUT THE AUTHOR

Dr. Roxanne Johnson DHA, MHA, BHS is a leader, coach, and mentor. She instills ethical leadership skills in those that she works with. She is the owner of Horizons, New Horizons for Our Communities.

http://linkedin.com/in/dr-roxanne-johnson-277233b2

https://www.facebook.com/Horizons-New-Horizons-for-Our-Communities-2263299057285780/

DAY 258 – STRENGTH

"I can do all things through Christ which strengtheneth me." - Philippians 4:13 (KJV)

There are situations in life when there are no explanations for the miracles that occur. When you are going through and not sure how you are going to make it, know that God is in control. My daughter is healing at an astonishing pace. As I look at my daughter today and see how far God has brought her, I know it was God!

_____

_____

_____

ABOUT THE AUTHOR

Dr. Roxanne Johnson DHA, MHA, BHS is a leader, coach, and mentor. She instills ethical leadership skills in those that she works with. She is the owner of Horizons, New Horizons for Our Communities.
http://linkedin.com/in/dr-roxanne-johnson-277233b2
https://www.facebook.com/Horizons-New-Horizons-for-Our-Communities-2263299057285780/

DAY 259 – YES, YOU ARE GOD'S GIFT

> "Then God looked over all God had made, and God saw that it was very good!" - Genesis 1:31

Women are constantly being reminded that somehow we have missed the mark. Constantly living up to others' standards and expectations can dampen our spirits. While personal development and growth are important, it is unfortunate that we don't realize just how acceptable we already are. Yes, your corny jokes or your attention to detail might annoy one person, but someone needs the joy or organization you bring. You are a gift.

_____

_____

_____

ABOUT THE AUTHOR

Dr. Banjo writes, and speaks on topics related to social identity, social perception, and cultural difference from an empathic viewpoint.
Omotayo Banjo
Cincinnati, Ohio
www.omotayobanjo.com

DAY 260 – ONE WOMAN'S JOURNEY, ANOTHER'S GPS

"Do nothing out of selfish ambition or vain conceit. Rather, in humility value others above yourselves." - Philippians 2:3

Choosing to see our value liberates us to see *others'* value. Too often, women see one another as competitors when we could be collaborators. The person we are gossiping about could very well be the answer to a problem we are facing. There may come a day where someone else's story navigates us through our own journey. Refusing to learn from someone else is a sure way to squander an opportunity to advance your life.

_____

_____

_____

ABOUT THE AUTHOR

Dr. Banjo writes, and speaks on topics related to social identity, social perception, and cultural difference from an empathic viewpoint.
Omotayo Banjo
Cincinnati, Ohio
www.omotayobanjo.com

DAY 261 — AWAKENING TO YOUR TRUE IDENTITY PART 1

"You Are Fearfully And Wonderfully Made" - Psalm 139:14

I work with and support women who have been affected by childhood abuse and trauma. These women are tired of feeling broken, ashamed, unloved, and burdened by the past. They are stuck and unable to move forward. They are saved, yet still bound.

When you awaken to your true identity as a child of God: a daughter of the King; you will unlock your destiny for the glory of His kingdom. Christ came to set the captives free.

_____

_____

_____

ABOUT THE AUTHOR

Helping women to heal from the effects of childhood abuse and trauma, by awakening them to their true identity, purpose and value in Christ.
Jewell Fairweather
Health and Wellness Coach
jewellfairweather@gmail.com

DAY 262 – AWAKENING TO YOUR TRUE IDENTITY PART 2

"You Are Fearfully And Wonderfully Made" - Psalm 139:14

When God created you, He knew what He was doing. He created a strong, powerful, and resilient replica of Himself - in His image and in His likeness. You have weathered the storms, tests and trials. You survived the hard places and proven your toughness. You are still here and standing.

He knew you before the foundation of the world. He blessed and anointed you and kept you such a Kairos time as this.

_____

_____

_____

ABOUT THE AUTHOR

Helping women to heal from the effects of childhood abuse and trauma, by awakening them to their true identity, purpose and value in Christ.
Jewell Fairweather
Health and Wellness Coach
jewellfairweather@gmail.com

DAY 263 – FIRST STEPS TO FINANCIAL FREEDOM

"The better we master our emotions the better we will manage our money." - Stacie L. Daniel

Self-awareness is key. Knowing your emotional triggers, your spending tendencies, and your strengths and weaknesses about money will help to break your unhealthy money patterns. Our emotions have a price tag. Emotional healing, pattern recognition, and planned alternate behaviors are the solutions. Try these short assignments:

- List three memories or events that lead you to comfort shopping.

- List three alternate things to do the next time your emotions get the best of you.

_____

_____

_____

ABOUT THE AUTHOR

Stacie L. Daniel ~ National Speaker | Author | Wealth Strategist | Insurance Broker
Lynwood, Illinois
Newest book, 8 Silent Wealth Killers
Teaching Small Business Owners, Solopreneurs, and Side Hustlers how to *grow*, *save*, *spend*, and *protect* their money.

DAY 264 – FACING YOUR FINANCIAL REALITY

"Personal finance is not common sense and effective money management is a skill that must be learned." -Stacie L. Daniel

Success in other areas cause us to believe we can successfully manage our money as well. Then, our pride and ego lend to years of suffering in silence. We learn so much about other things but are reluctant to admit we need to learn about money and how to make it work for us. Try these short assignments:

- List three areas of finance where you could use some clear direction.

- How would your life change if you sought help?

_____

_____

_____

ABOUT THE AUTHOR

Stacie L. Daniel ~ National Speaker | Author | Wealth Strategist | Insurance Broker
Lynwood, Illinois
Facebook/Instagram/LinkedIn @motivatingyourmoney
stacie@financialmotivations.com

DAY 265 — MISINFORMATION

"Not knowing is the reason why you are in this financial position today. Not acting will be the reason why you are in this same position tomorrow." - Stacie L. Daniel

Many people have been completely misinformed about money and how to make it work. Make the concepts below a priority. They will give you the keys needed to build, maintain, and pass on generational wealth.

- Personal finance has little to do with money.

- Retirement has nothing to do with age.

- Wealth is not determined by a dollar amount.

_____

_____

_____

ABOUT THE AUTHOR

Stacie L. Daniel ~ National Speaker | Author | Wealth Strategist | Insurance Broker
Lynwood, Illinois
The Motivating Your Money Radio Show
Airs Sundays and Wednesdays at 8:00 pm c.s.t.

DAY 266 – MONEY MINDSET MASTERY

"No matter where you have been, no matter what you have done, and no matter what your life looks like right now - A life **FREE** of financial worry is indeed possible." - Stacie L. Daniel

"Why weren't I taught about money at home, in church, in college, or on my corporate job?" I was angry but turned it into motivation and used it to fuel my next financial footsteps. That is when my situation began to change.

Here are the three truths I accepted about myself:

- I need to change how I handle my money.
- I cannot make these changes on my own. (I have tried.)
- I need to reach out to someone and ask for help.

_____

_____

_____

ABOUT THE AUTHOR

Stacie L. Daniel ~ National Speaker | Author | Wealth Strategist | Insurance Broker
Lynwood, Illinois
Facebook/Instagram/LinkedIn @motivatingyourmoney
stacie@financialmotivations.com

DAY 267 – TAXES

"Tax reduction and tax avoidance is not the same as tax evasion. They put you in jail for tax evasion.

They pat you on the back for knowing how to do the other two." - Stacie. L. Daniel

There are very powerful but hidden money rules that the wealthy have been using for several decades to protect & grow their money in plain sight. Fear of the unknown makes us disregard what we do not understand and we miss out on many opportunities. This is concept called "contempt prior to investigation" and it's very costly.

Write a list of the things you were told to never do with your money and their reasons. Then ask your trusted financial professional for the surprising truth.

_____

_____

_____

ABOUT THE AUTHOR

Stacie L. Daniel ~ National Speaker | Author | Wealth Strategist | Insurance Broker
Lynwood, Illinois
The Motivating Your Money Radio Show
Airs Sundays and Wednesdays at 8:00 pm c.s.t.

DAY 268 – LEARN POWERFUL BUT HIDDEN MONEY RULES

"Give yourself and immediate raise by paying attention to the money that you are giving away and the money that is being taken from you every day." - Stacie L. Daniel

After learning how to manage my finances, I began helping other people to do the same. Now, I show women how to get out of debt in nine years or less without it costing you any more money than what they are paying now. I show people how to receive monthly paychecks and "playchecks" when they retire - tax free, guaranteed, and lasted until death. People's lives and their future are changed after they learn how to make these ideas work for specifically for themselves.

_____

_____

_____

ABOUT THE AUTHOR

Stacie L. Daniel ~ National Speaker | Author | Wealth Strategist | Insurance Broker
Lynwood, Illinois
Newest book, 8 Silent Wealth Killers
Facebook/Instagram/LinkedIn @motivatingyourmoney
stacie@financialmotivations.com

DAY 269 – LIVE A LIFE BY DESIGN

"What would you do if you knew you could not fail?" - Unknown

We were not given a spirit of fear. Fear was passed down by those unaware of the power within them. For example, if you were never taught to secure a good job to support yourself how could you have dreams worth realizing? I dreamed of getting paid to pursue my passions and help others, and now I do. I help people to design a life of their choosing.

_____

_____

_____

ABOUT THE AUTHOR

Angela is the CEO and founder of Livity Escapes and Livity Wellness Solutions. She is a certified travel consultant and IIN certified health coach. Angela is also a certified registered nurse anesthetist.
Angela Billups
Washington, D.C.
www.livityescapes.com
Angela@livityescapes.com
Instagram/Facebook: @LivityEscapes
www.facebook.com/LivityEscapes

DAY 270 – HAVE PATIENCE WITH YOUR GOALS

"Better to be patient than powerful; better to have self-control than conquer a city." - Proverbs 16:32 (NLT)

We want success now, but rarely consider if we have the foundation necessary to support what we actually want. There are always shortcuts, but they seldom prepare us for the responsibilities of the next level. Patience is the long game with the greater gain. Through it, God molds us into who we need to be. Patience is a fruit of the Spirit. By exhibiting it, we show that we are His.

_____

_____

_____

ABOUT THE AUTHOR

Angela is the CEO and founder of Livity Escapes and Livity Wellness Solutions. She is a certified travel consultant and IIN certified health coach. Angela is also a certified registered nurse anesthetist.
Angela Billups
Washington, D.C.
www.livityescapes.com
Angela@livityescapes.com
Instagram/Facebook: @LivityEscapes
www.facebook.com/LivityEscapes

DAY 271 — BREAK FREE FROM THE NORM PART 1

"I am free because I know that I, alone, am morally responsible for everything I do. I am free, no matter what rules surround me. If I find them tolerable, I tolerate them; if I find them too obnoxious, I break them. I am free because I know that I, alone, am morally responsible for everything I do." - Robert A. Heinlein

I was raised to work hard, pay bills, go to college, and get a good paying job. I was also taught to get married and have kids. I had not learned how to keep myself free. The inability to heal from a repetitive cycle of failures kept me in shackles. Not until I was able to break through the cycles of life that kept me in bondage, did my true freedom ring.

_____

_____

_____

ABOUT THE AUTHOR

As a mom, "nana" and C.E.O, Wanda Barkley's lifestyle and leadership serves as an inspiration across many generations.
www.WanBarkfoundation.org
www.Eespreschool.com
Facebook - Earlyedpreschoolorlando
Instagram - Earlyeducationstationorlando

DAY 272 – BREAK FREE FROM THE NORM PART 2

"I am free because I know that I, alone, am morally responsible for everything I do. I am free, no matter what rules surround me. If I find them tolerable, I tolerate them; if I find them too obnoxious, I break them. I am free because I know that I, alone, am morally responsible for everything I do." - Robert A. Heinlein

I do not want the cute little house with the white picket fence. This is not in my DNA! Where is my mansion? They say, "Follow the yellow brick road!" Well I did, only to end up with that cute little house. My dreams were crashed in the midst of women all scrambling to break free too. Break free from the norm and embrace your uniqueness.

_____

_____

_____

ABOUT THE AUTHOR

Wanda Barkley
www.WanBarkfoundation.org
www.Eespreschool.com
Facebook - Earlyedpreschoolorlando
Instagram - Earlyeducationstationorlando

DAY 273 – REASSURING FAITH

"For with God nothing shall be impossible." - Luke 1:37

It is difficult to take the next steps when we cannot see the full staircase or the path ahead. Our basic instincts want certainty. God reassures us that with him all things are possible and when he accompanies us, there is nothing we cannot do. Faith does not ensure that things will be easy, but it makes them possible. Go forward in strength and stride in victory!

_____

_____

_____

ABOUT THE AUTHOR

Jerri is a counselor, professional business consultant, mentor and educator who enriches her community, clients and consumers through educational seminars and publications.
Jerri Reed-Taylor
Licensed Funeral Director & Embalmer Counselor
Educator Professional Business Consultant
jtaylorconsulting@yahoo.com
www.facebook.com/jerri.reed.357

DAY 274 – FAITH THAT WILL NOT FAIL

"God is within her, she will not fail." - Psalm 46:5

Trials test your faith while tests yield testimonies. I always worry that I could fail if I did not study and work hard. It is reassuring to know that when faced with adversity, God is not just standing by watching. He is in the midst of the situation enduring with you. Go forward knowing that God is not just nearby or around you, he is within you therfore you will not fail.

_____

_____

_____

ABOUT THE AUTHOR

Jerri is a counselor, professional business consultant, mentor and educator who enriches her community, clients and consumers through educational seminars and publications.
Jerri Reed-Taylor
Licensed Funeral Director & Embalmer Counselor
Educator Professional Business Consultant
jtaylorconsulting@yahoo.com
www.facebook.com/jerri.reed.357

DAY 275 – FAITH THAT IS HANDED TO YOU

"For I am the Lord your God who takes hold of your right hand and says to you, Do not fear; I will help you." - Isaiah 41:13

When my four-year-old daughter and I cross busy streets, I take her hand. It is natural response. As her mother, my instinct is to protect and guide her. God does the same for us. He takes our hand and says, "Do not fear." Our faith in God, shields us from danger. It ensures that we travel in the paths where he leads us.

_____

_____

_____

ABOUT THE AUTHOR

Jerri is a counselor, professional business consultant, mentor and educator who enriches her community, clients and consumers through educational seminars and publications.
Jerri Reed-Taylor
Licensed Funeral Director & Embalmer Counselor
Educator Professional Business Consultant
jtaylorconsulting@yahoo.com
www.facebook.com/jerri.reed.357

DAY 276 — FAITH IN WHAT I KNOW

"Now faith is the substance of things hoped for, the evidence of things not seen."
- Hebrews 11:1

People have been trusting God for thousands of years. Abraham was willing to sacrifice his only son at God's command. Our level of faith determines how we respond to God. Standing strong in his faith, Abraham's response was, "God will provide." Faith is being sure of what you desire and certain of what we do not see. Go forward in grace and have faith in what you already know!

_____

_____

_____

ABOUT THE AUTHOR

Jerri is a counselor, professional business consultant, mentor and educator who enriches her community, clients and consumers through educational seminars and publications.
Jerri Reed-Taylor
Licensed Funeral Director & Embalmer Counselor
Educator Professional Business Consultant
jtaylorconsulting@yahoo.com
www.facebook.com/jerri.reed.357

DAY 277 – IF YOU DON'T HAVE FAITH IN YOUR BUSINESS IT WILL REVEAL ITSELF IN YOUR ACTIONS - PART 1

"Now faith is the substance of things hoped for, the evidence of things not seen."
- Hebrews 11.1 (KJV)

You must have faith in your business. It will lead you to invest the time, energy, effort and finances it needs to sustain itself before any profits are made. You cannot expect others to invest in your business if you do not. This is what I call the "Vision Blocking Zone," where so many dreams sit idle and business visions rarely come to fruition.

_____

_____

_____

ABOUT THE AUTHOR

Annette is the CEO and founder of Dynamic Participators Enterprises, Inc. and the President of the Civilian Morale Welfare and Recreation association with over 3,000 military and civilian employees.
Annette Watson-Johnson B.A, M.S
www.dynamicparticipators.org
dynamicparticipators@gmail.com
Facebook & Instagram: @dynamicparticipators
Twitter: @dynamicparticipators1
YouTube Channel: dynamic participators

DAY 278 – IF YOU DON'T HAVE FAITH IN YOUR BUSINESS IT WILL REVEAL ITSELF IN YOUR ACTIONS - PART 2

"Now faith is the substance of things hoped for, the evidence of things not seen." - Hebrews 11.1 (KJV)

A business owner should always love what they do. I created a business that includes elements that I am passionate about. My personal experiences with my mental, physical and spiritual wellness led me to want to help others incorporate the same elements into their lives. I started a non-profit organization that specialize as wellness event planners with a primary focus on promoting and educating self-care regiments. We create inclusive wellness programs and events. We believe we are the ambassadors of wellness because "We do Wellness Well"

_____

_____

_____

ABOUT THE AUTHOR

Annette Watson-Johnson B.A, M.S
www.dynamicparticipators.org
dynamicparticipators@gmail.com
Facebook & Instagram: @dynamicparticipators
Twitter: @dynamicparticipators1
YouTube Channel: dynamic participators

DAY 279 — WHERE DREAMS AND VISION LIVE, PART 1 - PURPOSE

"But Daniel purposed in his heart..." - Daniel 1:8-9

Whatever is your desire, the first task is to get the dream the vision firmly fixed in your own heart. Only then will you continue to persevere in the face of tremendous odds, self-doubt, the discouragement of nay-sayers, and any real and tangible barriers. When your dream is set and your purpose clear, God will bring you into favor with those who can help bring your dream into fruition.

_____

_____

_____

ABOUT THE AUTHOR

Dr. Moore is a retired educator, author, independent speaker, trainer, and coach with the John Maxwell Team. She specializes in personal and professional growth and development.
Mary Webster Moore, Ph.D.
Chicago, Illinois
www.marywebstermoore.com
marymoorebusiness@gmail.com

DAY 280 – WHERE DREAMS AND VISION LIVE, PART 2 - NON-NEGOTIABLES

"... he would not defile himself with the king's meat..."   - Daniel 1:8-17)

Daniel's story is an interesting departure point for success in all areas of life. His faith could not be shaken by the threats before him. You must decide what are your non-negotiables. What you will and will not do. There must be places where you draw your line in the sand and stand. Integrity and an unyielding faith in God are keys to your success.

_____

_____

_____

ABOUT THE AUTHOR

Dr. Moore is a retired educator, author, independent speaker, trainer, and coach with the John Maxwell Team. She specializes in personal and professional growth and development.
Mary Webster Moore, Ph.D.
Chicago, Illinois
www.marywebstermoore.com
marymoorebusiness@gmail.com

DAY 281 – MONEY CAN'T BUY YOU LOVE - PART 1

"God won't give you more than you can handle"   - 1 Corinthians 10:13

Being a person who worked most of my life, I never really wanted for anything. One thing I learned was money can't buy love. Love, without God's invitation, goes nowhere. With the help of God when you are building a relationship, things will work itself out. You trust more and move as one. When you are role playing and the answers are all wrong, again, listen to God.

_____

_____

_____

ABOUT THE AUTHOR

Kym is an army veteran and owner of Beach Girls PR and Marketing. She has a degree in public relations and pursuing her masters of business administration (MBA) at Southern New Hampshire University (SNHU).
Kym Oglesby
Panama City, Florida
info@beachgirlspr.com

DAY 282 – MONEY CAN'T BUY YOU LOVE - PART 2

"God won't give you more than you can handle." - 1 Corinthians 10:13

God is a loving God, but a jealous one too. I thought I could buy happiness, but it just materialize into a huge bill. After I realized what happen, I asked myself, "Girl, how did you get here?" I remember just wanting to be different. Yet, I was different. God blessed me to see that I was not the same. I have traveled around the world and have lived a dream life. God's love makes me laugh, live a better life and love myself even more.

_____

_____

_____

ABOUT THE AUTHOR

Kym is an army veteran and owner of Beach Girls PR and Marketing. She has a degree in public relations and pursuing her masters of business administration (MBA) at Southern New Hampshire University (SNHU).
Kym Oglesby
Panama City, Florida
info@beachgirlspr.com

DAY 283 – STEPPING OUT OF YOUR COMFORT ZONE

"For I know the plans I have for you, declares the Lord, plans for welfare and not to harm you, plans to give you hope and a future." - Jeremiah 29:11

On this journey of faith we surrender all hope's, dreams, aspirations to Him, so we can have freedom from all bondages. Walking out of the familiar of comfort and stepping into greatness. We need to focus our attention on Him to lead, guide and direct our paths, our plans and our future goals. As we trust His will and His way we can have the desires of our hearts.

_____

_____

_____

ABOUT THE AUTHOR

Dena McCombs
Greenville, South Carolina
Https://m.facebook.com/MzsPeace

DAY 284 — YOUR ULTIMATE FREEDOM

"Freedom is about finding and loving yourself and knowing God through it all!"
- Kentra FuQua

Ultimate freedom is understanding your finances and your credit. It is the ability to save and to be independent from others. Once you have mastered these things, no one can get in your way! Know that nothing happens over night! It takes time. There is always room to grow and learn so just keep working on the best you, your career, your business and ultimately your best life. I had to learn this myself, the hard way. Especially when it comes to relationships. Although you have to be a team player, you should have your own life together and bring something to the table.

_____

_____

_____

ABOUT THE AUTHOR

Kentra Fuqua is a very strong and compensate women. After a very hard up bringing she pushed forward to obtain her bachelor's of science in business administration.
Kentra FuQua
Oakland, California
MsfuQua1999@gmail.com

DAY 285 – CURVE BALLS & GIGANTIC WALLS

"The greater the obstacle, the more glory in overcoming it." - Molière

Life obstacles do not have to stop you. Life will occasionally throw you a curve ball or a gigantic wall. When you run into a wall, do not turn around and give up! You can figure out how to climb it or even work around it. To conquer a life obstacle is always a great life accomplishment. Remember, there is glory on the other side.

_____

_____

_____

ABOUT THE AUTHOR

Jennifer Biggins is from Cordele, Georgia and resides in Ocala, Florida. She is a proud graduate of Lake Region high school. Jennifer is passionate about caring for children, whose families are in the middle of transitions.
DNW21@gmail.com
www.independentlydevelopinganewway.com
www.facebook.com/IDNW21
www.linkedin.com/in/idnw21
twitter.com/idnw21
www.instagram.com/idanw21

DAY 286 – THE BIGGER THE SETBACK, THE GREATER THE COMEBACK

"The wise woman builds her house, but with her own hands the foolish one tears her down." - Proverbs 14:1

When you set out to shatter glass ceilings, many will try to knock you down and few will lift you up. During these trying times, you must use negativity to fuel positivity. You will want to give up as you are being pulled down, but use this energy to fuel your greatest passions. In the end, you will build your house of dreams and fund your future dreams!

_____

_____

_____

ABOUT THE AUTHOR

LeAnne Salazar Montoya, ABD is from Medanales, New Mexico. She is an educator, professional development trainer, and CEO and founder of Salazar Creations Consulting.

www.linkedin.com/in/leanne87548
Twitter: @eeanntoya
https://www.portfoliogen.com/leanne87548
eeanntoya@gmail.com

DAY 287 — LIV'IN MY BEST LIFE - PART 1

"The world is a book, and those who do not travel read only one page." - Saint Augustine

Ask yourself are you really living the life you deserve or want? Don't be afraid to do something out of the ordinary and full of adventure. You have the power to break down the walls of your own conformity and shift your script. Just stop caring what others think and live your life your way. It is time to wake up friends, rise above the normal and revel in the abnormal.

_____

_____

_____

ABOUT THE AUTHOR

Yasna is a mother of two amazing children and a business owner of LivToast2Coast. She is an adventure seeker, hope giver, and champion of all those living life to the fullest. She works in corporate management.
Yasna Guneysu
Des Plaines, Illinois
https://www.facebook.com/groups/244989442367032/members/
https://www.facebook.com/yasna.guneysu
https://www.instagram.com/parispineapple/
https://twitter.com/yasna1guneysu
http://guneysu1.timetoliv.com|yasna.guneysu@gmail.com

DAY 288 – LIV'IN MY BEST LIFE PART 2

"Life is a blank canvas, and you need to throw all the paint on it you can." - Danny Kaye

We need people to help pave the wave to individuality and freedom.   Freedom of time is a gift that many of us seek yet do not have. You are worthy of adventures and discovering your true self. Travel with those you cherish and make new memories. God created us to see the world, connect, and make a difference in the lives we touch.   Go out and paint your world, and LIV free.

_____

_____

_____

ABOUT THE AUTHOR

Yasna is a mother of two amazing children and a business owner of LivToast2Coast. She is an adventure seeker, hope giver, and champion of all those living life to the fullest. She works in corporate management.
Yasna Guneysu
Des Plaines, Illinois
https://www.facebook.com/groups/244989442367032/members/
https://www.facebook.com/yasna.guneysu
https://www.instagram.com/parispineapple/
https://twitter.com/yasna1guneysu
http://guneysu1.timetoliv.com|yasna.guneysu@gmail.com

DAY 289 — HAVE A POSITIVE MINDSET

"Some blessings come soon, some come late, and some don't come until heaven; but for those who embrace the gospel of Jesus Christ, they come." Elder Holland, The Church of Jesus Christ of Latter-Day Saints

We, as women, should always have a grateful heart. We are blessed in so many ways, whether we are aware of them or not. There will be times when we question our faith or feel our prayers have not been answered. Our Heavenly Father knows and is aware of our life struggles. He knows our current situations and when we are ready, He will bless us. Be patient and know that He loves you.

_____

_____

_____

ABOUT THE AUTHOR

Dr. Cook's purpose is to not only motivate, inspire and entertain educators, but share practical, proven strategies they can take away and use effectively in their classrooms.
Amelia Cook, Ed.D.
Las Vegas, Nevada
www.educatewithaloha.com
educatewithaloha@gmail.com
|www.facebook.com/educatewithaloha

DAY 290 – NEVER TOO LATE TO CHANGE

"Every valley shall be filled, and every mountain and hill shall be brought low; and the crooked shall be made straight, and the rough ways shall be made smooth." - Luke 3:5

Every one of us is imperfect. We have all made mistakes and have made decisions we may not be proud of. Our Heavenly Father can help us straighten our crooked paths by admitting our wrongs and living a life that chooses right. It is never too late to change. It is never too late to have a fresh, new view about life, about God, and about one's self. Having an open heart and an open mind will allow us to truly receive the Lord and be happy.

_____

_____

_____

ABOUT THE AUTHOR

Dr. Cook's purpose is to not only motivate, inspire and entertain educators, but share practical, proven strategies they can take away and use effectively in their classrooms.
Amelia Cook, Ed.D.
Las Vegas, Nevada
www.educatewithaloha.com
educatewithaloha@gmail.com
|www.facebook.com/educatewithaloha

DAY 291 – WHEN ALL ELSE FAILS, KEEP THE FAITH - PART 1

"Trust in the Lord with all your heart and lean not on your own understanding; in all your ways submit to him and he will make your path straight." - Proverbs 3:5-6 (NIV)

Webster's Dictionary defines faith as the complete trust and confidence in someone or something. Our someone is God, and the something are God's promises. God is never concerned about the size of our faith except that we have at least a mustard seed faith. A mustard seed is not big at all so breakthroughs and miracles are never dependent on the size of our faith but it is great when we have it.

_____

_____

_____

ABOUT THE AUTHOR

After spending twenty five years in education, Michelle' is a caregiver, Godmother, motivational speaker, mentor, author, actress, plus size model, entrepreneur, and community leader.
Michelle' (Bunny) R. Scoggins M.Ed., Ed.S.
Doctoral Candidate
San Antonio, Texas
www.screamsfromthechurchpewmichelle.info
www.facebook.com/AuthorBunny
Instagram - bunnys06 |Twitter - @BunnyScoggins

DAY 292 – WHEN ALL ELSE FAILS, KEEP THE FAITH - PART 2

"Trust in the Lord with all your heart and lean not on your own understanding; in all your ways submit to him and he will make your path straight." - Proverbs 3:5-6 (NIV)

We all wake up and have the best intentions of having a good day. One obstacle after the other seems to happen from the moment we wake up. We all have had bad days, and hard times When we keep our eyes on God and our faith rooted on the solid rock, everything else around us can be sinking sand. He wakes us up and knows what we will face before we do. Decide if you will be bitter or better? The victim or victor?

_____

_____

_____

ABOUT THE AUTHOR

After spending twenty five years in education, Michelle' is a caregiver, Godmother, motivational speaker, mentor, author, actress, plus size model, entrepreneur, and community leader.
Michelle' (Bunny) R. Scoggins M.Ed., Ed.S.
Doctoral Candidate
San Antonio, Texas
www.screamsfromthechurchpewmichelle.info
www.facebook.com/AuthorBunny
Instagram - bunnys06 |Twitter - @BunnyScoggins

DAY 293 – THE COMEBACK

"Come back to the place of safety, all you prisoners who still have hope! I promise this very day that I will repay two blessings for each of your troubles." - Zechariah 9:12

Sister, your comeback is going to be greater than the devastation of the derailing that sidelined you. He is going to use the scraps from the years the cankerworm has eaten and the ashes from the time wasted as fuel for your engine. It is not over. All is not lost. Remember, He started this work in you and He will be faithful to complete it.

Are you ready to lock it in and go forth, full speed ahead?

_____

_____

_____

ABOUT THE AUTHOR

Sonja R. Pickett
Sanford, Florida
www.facebook.com/mrs.pickett

DAY 294 – STRIVING TO OPTIMIZE OUR POTENTIAL

"Together we can make changes." - Myron Scott

One of my core beliefs is that all people are to be valued and offered every opportunity to reach their full potential.

To be successful in what you do, you need to know what skills you have so you can optimize them. As you become aware of your skills, grant others the opportunity to become aware of theirs. We can support each other to maximize our potential for our benefit, as well as others. Let us wisely make use of every opportunity.

_____

_____

_____

ABOUT THE AUTHOR

Ms. Myron L. Scott, MS, MA, BCBA Board Certified Behavior Analyst Founder/CEO of Omega Behavior Analysis, LLC.
Myron Scott
Ocala, Florida
http://omegabehavior.com/index.html
office@omegabehavior.com

DAY 295 – FREEDOM OF HEALTH - CHANGE YOUR LIFE

"We spend the first half of our lives to gain wealth. We spend the second half of our lives to gain health." - Voltaire 18th Century

We can desire freedom in many areas of our lives but if we are lacking in our health, freedom is of no importance. We all desire freedom from disease, pain and agony to enjoy our lives. Proper blood flow is vital to health to ensure proper supply of nutrients and oxygen. On this basis, it is clear the critical role the circulatory system plays in overall health. To get your life back is priceless.

_____

_____

_____

ABOUT THE AUTHOR

I am passionate about sharing the freedom of health, honoring our bodies as the temple of the Holy Spirit and understanding that our bodies have the innate ability to heal themselves.
Cindy Timmins
www.cindytimmins.com
www.LifeByDesign.BemerGroup.com

DAY 296 – FREEDOM IN HEALTH - FEARFULLY AND WONDERFULLY MADE.

"I will praise you. I am fearfully and wonderfully made...." - Psalm 139:14

You my God, created my innermost being. You knit me together in my mother's womb. Your works are wonderful. What freedom to live in health to glorify God with our bodies.

I know my body is the temple of The Holy Spirit that lives within me. I am not my own. I was bought with a price. Therefore I have the freedom to live a disease-free life. I have freedom to live energized and to live without pain. I have freedom to enjoy life in good health.

_____

_____

_____

ABOUT THE AUTHOR

Cindy Timmins
www.cindytimmins.com
www.LifeByDesign.BemerGroup.com
https://www.facebook.com/cindytimmins
https://twitter.com/cindytimmins
https://www.youtube.com/user/cindytimmins
http://cindytimmins.blogspot.com/
https://www.linkedin.com/in/cindytimmins/
https://www.pinterest.com/cindywt/
https://www.instagram.com/healthprenuer/

DAY 297 – HAVE FAITH. HAVE FREEDOM. HAVE SUCCESS PART 1

"Stand fast therefore in the liberty wherewith Christ has made us free, and be not entangled again with the yoke of bondage." – Galations 5:1

Being faith-filled and living fear-free equals freedom and success. When measuring success, we all have our own view of how it should be defined. One fact that I have learned from my struggles, triumphs and endeavors is that real success requires real effort and accountability. Do you believe you have the right tools to exceed your goals? Leaning into a support to help you with goal achievment is a solid choice in moving forward.

_____

_____

_____

ABOUT THE AUTHOR

Jennifer Yon, CEO of Jennifer Yon Agency and IBA Success Magazine the official publication of Jennifer Yon Agency.
www.JenniferYon.com
pr@JenniferYon.com

DAY 298 – HAVE FAITH. HAVE FREEDOM. HAVE SUCCESS PART 2

"Stand fast therefore in the liberty wherewith Christ has made us free, and be not entangled again with the yoke of bondage." – Galations 5:1

Helping individuals realize, strategize and execute their dreams embodies my greatest labor of love. Whether you are an established or desiring CEO, there will be times when you feel you are on a roller coaster and you will question what to do next. When you develop a network of valuable resources, or "tool box," you are in a greater position to operate your business more efficiently, increase your revenue, and invest in your skills - all while doing what you love.

_____

_____

_____

ABOUT THE AUTHOR

Jennifer Yon, CEO of Jennifer Yon Agency and IBA Success Magazine the official publication of Jennifer Yon Agency.
www.JenniferYon.com
pr@JenniferYon.com

DAY 299 – DARE TO DESIGN AND LIVE THE LIFE YOU WANT!

"For I am about to do something new."- Isaiah 43:19 NLT

As a Life Coach, I love empowering people to design and live their best lives. I am passionate about developing talent, mentoring, and empowering women with business resource. When they succeed, I succeed. So, dare to design and live the life you want!" Life's too short to live unhappy. The past will haunt you if you let it. What binds you? Decide that Gods love will be your "refresh" button.

_____

_____

_____

ABOUT THE AUTHOR

Luz Morales, CEO FigAmora Global
Sanford, Florida
www.FigAmoraGlobal.com
FigAmoraGlobal@gmail.com
www.Myvortex365.com/figamoratravel
Youravon.com/Dnlglamspot

DAY 300 – DARE TO DREAM AGAIN

"And Joseph dreamed a dream, and he told *it* his brethren: and they hated him yet the more." - Genesis 37: 5 Read 45:4-12

Have you ever shared your dreams and had them crushed by words such as "you want to do what?!" Words have such weight and power to either crush or empower us. The truth is there is nothing impossible for you. God gives us the strength and ability to dream and do the unimaginable. Look at how Joseph, the dreamer sold to slaves, became an incredible ruler.

What have you written off as an impossible dream? Write a letter to yourself: what does it feel like when your dreams come true. What actions steps will you take today make them happen?

_____

_____

_____

ABOUT THE AUTHOR

Luz Morales, CEO FigAmora Global
Sanford, Florida
www.FigAmoraGlobal.com
FigAmoraGlobal@gmail.com
www.Myvortex365.com/figamoratravel
Youravon.com/Dnlglamspot

DAY 301 — JUST JUMP

"Just Do It" - Nike Brand

What is the scariest thing you can imagine yourself doing? The thing that has been in the back of your mind forever, but you have not done because you fear people's judgement? Guess what? Just do it. You only live once. If and when you fall, you can always get back up. My dream was to become a model. I have always been the backstage master of all trades. So, I just did it; I modeled! It was grand with my curvy tall fourty-five year young Latin woman in a shiny silver dress. I almost tripped on the runway and it was awesome. I went up and down the escalators modeling my heart out. If I can do it, so can you!

Your turn... What's your dream? Yes, that one. The one that you don't even dare to say out loud, Go do it, just jump!

_____

_____

_____

ABOUT THE AUTHOR

Luz Morales, CEO FigAmora Global
Sanford, Florida
www.FigAmoraGlobal.com
FigAmoraGlobal@gmail.com
www.Myvortex365.com/figamoratravel
Youravon.com/Dnlglamspot

DAY 302 – CRAFTED POWERFULLY IN HAS HAND

"Let love be without dissimulation. Abhor that which is evil; cleave to that which is good. Be kindly affectioned one to another with brotherly love; in honor preferring one another." - Romans 12:9-10

As I opened the door, I saw him, holding himself at the edge of the bed unable to talk and pale. He was having a second stroke. After abandoning me for five months, the day he returned he had a stroke. What do you do when the unimaginable happens? When the person who has shattered your heart needs you to basically save theirs? You help. God ALWAYS gives us the power to overcome!

What is your broken moment? Write down three things that you learned about yourself from your experience. Thank God for helping you recognize your inner strength. You are crafted powerfully by his hand.

_____

_____

_____

ABOUT THE AUTHOR

Luz Morales, CEO FigAmora Global
Sanford, Florida
www.FigAmoraGlobal.com
FigAmoraGlobal@gmail.com
www.Myvortex365.com/figamoratravel
Youravon.com/Dnlglamspot

DAY 303 – HE HAS INCREDIBLE PLANS FOR OUR FUTURE

"For I know the thoughts that I think toward you, saith the LORD, thoughts of peace, and not of evil, to give you an expected end." - Jeremiah 29: 11

At that moment I saw blood. I knew I was losing my baby. After fourty-two years of longing for a family of my own, it was all gone in a matter of few seconds. My fiancé was gone right after that. He went to find himself and he hasn't found his way back. We don't always understand why things happen. God has such a better future and hope for our lives regardless of the matters that are in front of us. I'm unsure of what direction my life is taking but I'm going to continue riding the wave of trust.

As you look at your life, is it what you expected? What events caused a shift in your life? Pray and make a plan to look for ways to add layers of joy to your life, because God design us to live life to the fullest.

_____

_____

_____

ABOUT THE AUTHOR

Luz Morales, CEO FigAmora Global
Sanford, Florida
www.FigAmoraGlobal.com
FigAmoraGlobal@gmail.com
www.Myvortex365.com/figamoratravel
Youravon.com/Dnlglamspot

DAY 304 — YOU ARE NEVER IN THE DARK FOR TOO LONG...

"The First Steps towards getting somewhere is to decide that you are not going to stay where you are" - Unknown

It was 1 o'clock in the morning and pitch black on the Florida-Turnpike with a flat tire. AAA could not figure out where we were so they could send a truck to pick us up. The decision was to cry or laugh, so we laughed and figured out how to direct the AAA people to us. When you are left out in the dark, stop, breath find the humor in the situation then you will find the way!

When was the last time you were in a tough spot where you felt helpless? What was your attitude? What have you discovered about your character and will you change?

_____

_____

_____

ABOUT THE AUTHOR

Luz Morales, CEO FigAmora Global
Sanford, Florida
www.FigAmoraGlobal.com
FigAmoraGlobal@gmail.com
www.Myvortex365.com/figamoratravel
Youravon.com/Dnlglamspot

DAY 305 — ADULTING

"Who can find a virtuous woman? for her price is far above rubies." - Proverbs 31:10

"Pay the bills, manage housework, pick up his cloths, kids-practice, oh, and this week, the dog is sick." Life is overwhelming. Who said life was easy? And how did that chica in Proverbs 31 do it? Good grief!! Adulating, really!!! She did well because she relied on God, to guide her through wisdom and she planned well.

Who do you rely on? How do you handle life and adulthood? You are not alone... Write three people that you can go to for counseling for tough decisions, then thank them.

_____

_____

_____

ABOUT THE AUTHOR

Luz Morales, CEO FigAmora Global
Sanford, Florida
www.FigAmoraGlobal.com
FigAmoraGlobal@gmail.com
www.Myvortex365.com/figamoratravel
Youravon.com/Dnlglamspot

DAY 305 – IT'S COFFEE TIME! I NEED STARBUCKS!!

Coffee+friends = love and laughter!!!

"Hand over my coffee and you won't get hurt!" - Unknown

Aaaah! I need coffee! There's that moment, where we need to vent because the world is falling apart, and we just realized we haven't had a mug of mocha yet. The truth is, we need weekly quality time to unwind. Maybe it's coffee time with your best bud, margaritas with work friends, or maybe it is taking a little walk with your best bud pup (mine is Flippy). Find the time to unwind.

Who are your vent best friends? You know, the ones that keep your world flowing. Pray for their needs and thank God for them.

_____

_____

_____

ABOUT THE AUTHOR

Luz Morales, CEO FigAmora Global
Sanford, Florida
www.FigAmoraGlobal.com
FigAmoraGlobal@gmail.com
www.Myvortex365.com/figamoratravel
Youravon.com/Dnlglamspot

DAY 306 — RISING TO THE CHALLENGE PART 1

"But thanks be to God! He gives us the victory through our Lord Jesus Christ"- 1 Corinthians 15:57

My faith was tested the most about three months ago, after the sudden passing of my sister. I was with her all week until two days before she was called home, and none of us expected this to happen. I am a bodybuilder, and I was in the middle of preparing for a national competition in Florida. My sister was my biggest supporter. Once she passed I had so much to get done in a small amount of time, but God got me through it all.

_____

_____

_____

ABOUT THE AUTHOR

Samantha is a juvenile probation officer with a passion for helping troubled youth. She has a bachelor degree in criminal justice, and a master degree in social work. She uses her bodybuilding to inspire others while striving toward her goals.
Samantha Simpson
www.facebook.com/samantha.s.simpson.9
@sammyboo32

DAY 307 — RISING TO THE CHALLENGE PART 2

"I planned her service, moved her things out of her apartment, and tied all of her loose ends, all while working full time and continuing to train for my competition. I felt so lost without my sister and best friend. Through prayer and the gym, I found peace. I competed in the biggest competition in the country, in loving memory of my sister. Five months of blood, sweat, and tears paid off once I was announced the first place winner. Though I was full of grief and anger, I continued to pray, trust God, and run my race.

_____

_____

_____

ABOUT THE AUTHOR

Samantha is a juvenile probation officer with a passion for helping troubled youth. She has a bachelor degree in criminal justice, and a master degree in social work. She uses her bodybuilding to inspire others while striving toward her goals.
Samantha Simpson
www.facebook.com/samantha.s.simpson.9
@sammyboo32

DAY 308 – BE A PERSON OF EXCELLENCE

"Whatever you do, do your work heartily, as for Lord rather than for men, knowing that from the Lord you will receive the reward of the inheritance. It's the Lord Christ whom you serve." - Colossians 3:23-24

Many people want to do as little as possible and still get by. Mediocrity is not of God. He doesn't want us to barely get by, or to do what everyone else is doing. God has called us to be people of excellence and integrity. You represent Almighty God. How you live, work and conduct your business, all reflects onto our God. Live your best life now, always aim for excellence.

_____

_____

_____

ABOUT THE AUTHOR

Ms. Myron L. Scott, MS, MA, BCBA Board Certified Behavior Analyst Founder/CEO of Omega Behavior Analysis, LLC.
Myron Scott
Ocala, Florida
http://omegabehavior.com/index.html
office@omegabehavior.com

DAY 309 — AGAINST ALL ODDS

"I can do all things through Christ which strengtheneth me." - Philippians 4:13

Growing up I spent half my life in the hospital. My health was very poor as I was born with a disease. I lived a childhood and teenage years not under the best of conditions.

I was told I would die through pregnancy and childbirth. I thought no man would marry me. I've been married 23 years and have five children. God is using me to impact women globally through my story of resilience.

What have you been told you cannot do. You can live above your limitations. You can thrive against all odds.

_____

_____

_____

ABOUT THE AUTHOR

Pamela Mantey
Www.glownetwork.org
https://www.facebook.com/GlowWomensNetwork/
https://www.facebook.com/groups/GLOWWOMENSNETWORK/?ref=share
Pam@glownetwork.org

DAY 310 – YOU ARE LIMITLESS

"Ye are of God, little children, and have overcome them: because greater is he that is in you, than he that is in the world." - l John 4:4

From your childhood until now, people who crossed paths in your life have either contributed negatively or positively to your self-perception. You relinquish your power when you let someone's words or perception of you shape and determine the trajectory of your future. Remember that He that is in you is greater. This means you are limitless in what you can accomplish what you put your mind to.

_____

_____

_____

ABOUT THE AUTHOR

Pamela Mantey
Www.glownetwork.org
https://www.facebook.com/GlowWomensNetwork/
https://www.facebook.com/groups/GLOWWOMENSNETWORK/?ref=share
Pam@glownetwork.org

DAY 311 – NURTURE YOURSELF NATURALLY

"Taking care of yourself doesn't necessarily mean 'me first,' it means 'me too.'" - Chimerre Lawrence

What do you do when nurturing yourself doesn't come easy? I've had to come face to face with this question in my journey to self-love and evolving into the woman that I am now. I've learned what it takes to keep my cup full and the frequency with which it needs to be filled. This process requires self-reflection, self-awareness and the ability to enforce healthy boundaries.

_____

_____

_____

ABOUT THE AUTHOR

Chimerre Lawrence, CPA
Deltona, Florida
Email: chimerrea@gmail.com
www.linkedin.com/in/chimerrelawrence

DAY 312 – YOUR FREEDOM IS WAITING

"For his anger *endureth but* a moment; in his favour *is* life: weeping may endure for a night, but joy *cometh* in the morning." - Psalm 30:5

Freedom is an essential component of being undeniable. Freedom is about no pressure, having clarity, exercising good habits and taking care of self. So, when I read that, "Freedom is to ask for nothing and expect nothing," off of a notepad one day, I thought, "No!" That is not right. When we put our vision out into the universe, we should be able to see, taste and feel the freedom coming.

_____

_____

_____

ABOUT THE AUTHOR

An International Best-Selling Author for her book Undeniable You 7 Steps To Soar. Certified Personal Development Life Coach. Entrepreneur and CEO of Myrtha Dubois Coaching & Consulting.
Myrtha Dubois, Clearwater Florida
www.myrthadubois.com
https://m.facebook.com/groups/undeniableyou
@myrthaduboiscoachingconsulting
Instagram - @myrtha_dubois

DAY 313 – YOUR FREEDOM IS UNDENIABLE

"For no one can lay a foundation other than that which is laid, which is Jesus Christ." - 1 Corinthians 3:11

Freedom is to believe you are deserving. Therefore, Freedom is about asking for everything and expecting it all. Be ready for the new you. Focus on all you need, want and desire. Write them down.

Next, examine what you already have, what your resources are, and in whom your support lies. Take action.

Give no excuses. Have no fear or doubt.

_____

_____

_____

ABOUT THE AUTHOR

An International Best-Selling Author for her book Undeniable You 7 Steps To Soar. Certified Personal Development Life Coach. Entrepreneur and CEO of Myrtha Dubois Coaching & Consulting.
Myrtha Dubois, Clearwater Florida
www.myrthadubois.com
https://m.facebook.com/groups/undeniableyou
@myrthaduboiscoachingconsulting
Instagram - @myrtha_dubois

DAY 314 – HIS GRACE IS SUFFICIENT

"And he said unto me, My grace is sufficient for thee: for my strength is made perfect in weakness. Most gladly therefore will I rather glory in my infirmities, that the power of Christ may rest upon me." - 2 Corinthians 12:9

His grace becomes sufficient in your weakness and struggles. In Paul's deficiencies, persecutions, and pain, God reassured him. He is doing the same for you. Grace is not a feeling it's an enablement. Your struggles may not go away, but His grace will sustain you. In any area you are struggling thank God for His grace. Whether it is your health, marriage, business, children, financial or other areas His grace is sufficient.

_____

_____

_____

ABOUT THE AUTHOR

Pamela Mantey
Www.glownetwork.org
https://www.facebook.com/GlowWomensNetwork/
https://www.facebook.com/groups/GLOWWOMENSNETWORK/?ref=share
Pam@glownetwork.org

DAY 315 – THE LAST WILL BE FIRST PART 1

"But many who are first will be last, and many who are last will be first." - Matthew 19:30

Start small, think big but always start with the end in mind. That is not only the approach I used to climb the corporate ladder, it is a proven strategy that can be applied to wealth development.

As an everyday woman, I once shied away from asking questions others seemed to know the answers to. Certain demographics just seemed to be born knowing what career paths would earn six figure salaries. They started with the end in mind, knowing the importance of compound interest. Start with the end in mind from today!

_____

_____

_____

ABOUT THE AUTHOR

Maureen Carnakie-Baker, MBA, PMP is an author and advocate for financial wellbeing. She is a consultant in the financial and healthcare technology industry.
Instagram: BakersFortune
www.FortuneTellHer.com
LinkedIn: http://www.linkedin.com/in/carnakiebaker

DAY 316 – THE LAST WILL BE FIRST PART 2

"But many who are first will be last, and many who are last will be first." - Matthew 19:30

The demographic I referred to seems to have an understanding of pension plans, 401ks and the importance of investing while young, even if it was only $25 a week.

My goal is to make that demographic more inclusive. My platform: Fortune Tell Her, targets helping women get past self-imposed stigmas associated with lack of knowledge and exposure and the thought that they need a large bank account to get started on the road to building wealth. Let's start on that road together and fast track it with the end in mind.

_____

_____

_____

ABOUT THE AUTHOR

Maureen Carnakie-Baker, MBA, PMP is an author and advocate for financial wellbeing. She is a consultant in the financial and healthcare technology industry.
Instagram: BakersFortune
www.FortuneTellHer.com
LinkedIn: http://www.linkedin.com/in/carnakiebaker

DAY 317 — I AM CHANGE

"Change will not come if we wait for some other person or some other time. We are the ones we've been waiting for. We are the change that we seek." - Barack Obama

Who am I? I am spirit! Who am I waiting on? The "I Am." Change starts on the inside: in my center, in my core, and in my truth. I am change. I am nature and I change with every season. I am change. I am always growing and shifting, then learning the lessons from every experience and circumstance. I am change! Who are you? I know who I am. I am you too.

_____

_____

_____

ABOUT THE AUTHOR

Lolita Thomas is a trainer, speaker, strategist, certified executive, money and business coach. She has extensive background in business development, training, professional coaching, and human development. Lolita coached over 6,000 people.
WakeUp Artist Lolita Thomas, master coach
WakeUp Now, LLC
wakeupcoachingnow@gmail.com
www.wakeupnowllc.com
https://www.facebook.com/WakeUpNowCoaching/

DAY 318 – CELEBRATE YOURSELF NOW AND FOREVER HOLD YOUR PEACE

"The more you praise and celebrate your life, the more there is in life to celebrate." - Oprah Winfrey

Today I will give myself freedom to celebrate myself from the inside out, loving every part of me! Starting with the greatest parts of me, then the parts I am growing into and last the parts I tell myself lies about and judge. I forgive myself and hold peace knowing I am worthy to be celebrated as I am!

_____

_____

_____

ABOUT THE AUTHOR

WakeUp Artist Lolita Thomas, Master Coach
WakeUp Now, LLC
wakeupcoachingnow@gmail.com
www.wakeupnowllc.com
www.facebook.com/WakeUpNowCoaching/

DAY 319 – WHAT SIZE AM I?

"If you want to make a permanent change, stop focusing on the size of your problems and start focusing on the size of you!" - T. Harv Eker

I am a giant! I am an ant! I am a human! Does size matter? Size only matters when it comes to you and no one else. What am I focusing on and do I have a choice on what I focus my attention on? Yes. My freedom comes from what I am focusing on, not the actual circumstance. My permanent change is to focus source my power and the size of me.

_____

_____

_____

ABOUT THE AUTHOR

WakeUp Artist Lolita Thomas, Master Coach
WakeUp Now, LLC
wakeupcoachingnow@gmail.com
www.wakeupnowllc.com
www.facebook.com/WakeUpNowCoaching/

DAY 320 – I AM FEMININE LEADERSHIP

"As we look ahead into the next century, leaders will be those who empower others." -- Bill Gates

I am only as great as my weakest link in my family and community. I am today's Feminine Leader and it is my commitment to ensure that session happens. It begins and ends with me. I am here to empower those who are open and want to take the baton and run the next leg of the race of transformation and growth.

_____

_____

_____

ABOUT THE AUTHOR

WakeUp Artist Lolita Thomas, Master Coach
WakeUp Now, LLC
wakeupcoachingnow@gmail.com
www.wakeupnowllc.com
www.facebook.com/WakeUpNowCoaching/

DAY 321 – THERE IS NO PLACE LIKE HOME!

"She considers a field and buys it; out of her earnings she plants a vineyard." - Proverbs 31:16 (NIV)

Real estate is a great investment and way of creating generational wealth. Leave a legacy for your children. Talk to a trusted real estate professional and lender to get preapproved to know your options. Besides tax deductions you get peace of mind knowing you and your family have a secure place of dwelling.

_____

_____

_____

ABOUT THE AUTHOR

Doxie Jelks
Cleveland, Ohio
www.MakeClevelandHome.com
doxiejelks@kw.com
linkedin.com/in/doxiejelks
facebook.com/ClevelandOHRealtor

DAY 322 – GET RID OF THAT DEBT!

"The rich rules over the poor, and the borrower is the slave of the lender." - Proverbs 22:7 (ESV)

Start with the bill with the smallest balance and pay it off. Keep paying off credit cards and other debt until you are debt free. Not only will your credit score increase but you will be able to buy a home with a much lower interest rate making your house note manageable.

_____

_____

_____

ABOUT THE AUTHOR

Doxie Jelks
Cleveland, Ohio
www.MakeClevelandHome.com
doxiejelks@kw.com
linkedin.com/in/doxiejelks
facebook.com/ClevelandOHRealtor

DAY 323 – DON'T BE AFRAID TO SHINE

"Ye are the light of the world. A city that is set on an hill cannot be hid. Neither do men light a candle, and put it under a bushel, but on a candlestick; and it giveth light unto all that are in the house." - Matthew 5:14-15

Fill the blank, I am amazing at_____. Was that hard? Sometimes it is hard to self-promote. Lack of recognition of our talents can make us miss out on job and promotional opportunities. What are three things that people consistently compliment you on? How can you translate these to a talent that helps you in the future? It takes courage to believe in yourself and own your talents as much as God believes in us. Take time to pray, thanking God for your talents and He give you the courage to shine.

_____

_____

_____

ABOUT THE AUTHOR

Luz Morales
Sanford, Florida
www.FigAmoraGlobal.com
FigAmoraGlobal@gmail.com
www.Myvortex365.com/figamoratravel
Youravon.com/Dnlglamspot

DAY 324 – OPEN-MINDEDNESS TO WEALTH CREATION

"If somebody offers you an amazing opportunity but you are not sure you can do it, say yes – then learn how to do it later!" - Richard Branson

It is said that most multimillionaires have multiple streams of income. If you want to elevate yourself to that income bracket, you also need to invest in multiple streams of incomes especially passive income. The interesting observation is that wealthy people do not turn away from money making opportunities. However, there are many people who are going from paycheck to paycheck who would not have an open mind to consider an opportunity.

_____

_____

_____

ABOUT THE AUTHOR

Pamela Mantey is the CEO of It Takes Money Honey Network, a platform promoting individuals and giving income creating resources.
www.ittakesmoneyhoney.com
https://www.facebook.com/ittakesmoneyhoneymagazine/
https://www.facebook.com/ittakesmoneyhoney/
Pamela@ittakesmoneyhoney.com

DAY 325 – THE DIFFERENCE BETWEEN PASSIVE AND RESIDUAL INCOME

"Everyday is a bank account, and time is our currency. No one is rich, no one is poor, we've got 24 hours each." – Christopher Rice

Passive income is money that is earned from a business that has little or no ongoing effort involved. Therefore once you invest, you keep getting paid long after the initial investment.

Rental property, ATM machine, dividend-producing stocks, Royalties on book sales, Digital Contents, Product Distribution, Affiliates Programs and more are examples of passive income. With residual income like direct sales, you receive good income as long as you're working and putting effort into it. You need both income types.

_____

_____

_____

ABOUT THE AUTHOR

Pamela Mantey is the CEO of It Takes Money Honey Network, a platform promoting individuals and giving income creating resources.
www.ittakesmoneyhoney.com
https://www.facebook.com/ittakesmoneyhoneymagazine/
https://www.facebook.com/ittakesmoneyhoney/
Pamela@ittakesmoneyhoney.com

DAY 326 – TIME IS MONEY PART 1

"Everyday is a bank account, and time is our currency. No one is rich, no one is poor, we've got 24 hours each." – Christopher Rice

We all have 24 hours. So how come some are rich and some are poor. The rich have a mastery in high performance activities and high yielding investments. You have to master, leverage and monetize what you already have and outsource what you do not. You must be selling something every day. You do not have to work hard but work smart by investing in passive and residual income.

_____

_____

_____

ABOUT THE AUTHOR

Pamela Mantey is the CEO of It Takes Money Honey Network, a platform promoting individuals and giving income creating resources.
www.ittakesmoneyhoney.com
https://www.facebook.com/ittakesmoneyhoneymagazine/
https://www.facebook.com/ittakesmoneyhoney/
Pamela@ittakesmoneyhoney.com

DAY 327 – TIME IS MONEY PART 2

Everyday is a bank account, and time is our currency. No one is rich, no one is poor, we've got 24 hours each. – Christopher Rice

How to sell every day: If you have a job, it is your salary or wages per hour. If you have a business, it is your profits divided by how many hours worked. We have 168 hours in a week. If your job is 40 hours a week, sleep time 56 hours, family time 14 hours etc. Calculate the number of hours you spend on different activities. Subtract all that from 168. Most people have about 30 - 40 to start another business. Do this exercise & invest your time wisely.

_____

_____

_____

ABOUT THE AUTHOR

Pamela Mantey is the CEO of It Takes Money Honey Network, a platform promoting individuals and giving income creating resources.
www.ittakesmoneyhoney.com
https://www.facebook.com/ittakesmoneyhoneymagazine/
https://www.facebook.com/ittakesmoneyhoney/
Pamela@ittakesmoneyhoney.com

DAY 328 – FAITH INTENSIFIED

"I can do all this through him who gives me strength." - Philippians 4:13

Everyday I ask God for wisdom and clarity of my Kingdom assignment. In the answer, I recognize my vision is bigger than I thought. Making my vision a reality, I took on numerous opportunities to minister through speaking, with many reaping the benefits of my knowledge. However, I was disappointed to realize I was mostly speaking for free. My revelation was that there is nothing wrong with being compensated for serving in your gift.

_____

_____

_____

ABOUT THE AUTHOR

Roxanne Robinson
Atlanta, Georgia
Kgigroup471@gmail.com
Facebook - Roxanneonamissionrobinson

DAY 329 – A DIVINE SHIFT

"But thanks be to God! He gives us the victory through our Lord Jesus Christ." - I Corinthians 15:57 (NIV)

There I was, still in the same financial position. The revelation I received was simply, "A divine shift must take place, to accomplish what God called me to do in the kingdom and marketplace." As a people pleaser, I was my own worst enemy. My mind needed reprogramming. A shift to receive the abundance God had for me. My faith had to be coupled with God's favor.Now I have shifted from being in the same financial position. Are you ready for a shift?

_____

_____

_____

ABOUT THE AUTHOR

Roxanne Robinson
Atlanta, Georgia
Kgigroup471@gmail.com
Facebook - Roxanneonamissionrobinson

DAY 330 – FEAR HINDERS PROSPERITY

"For the Spirit God gave us does not make us timid, but gives us power, love and self-discipline." 2 Timothy 1:7 (NIV)

In order to have a faith relationship, I had to divorce fear. Faith is the substance of things hoped for. As an entrepreneur, ministry leader, business owner, we must intensify our faith in our walk God. If we are believing God for every provision, we must believe it will be given. Our faith cannot be weak; it must be strong. Regardless of circumstance or timing. Do not be moved.

_____

_____

_____

ABOUT THE AUTHOR

Roxanne Robinson
Atlanta, Georgia
Kgigroup471@gmail.com
Facebook - Roxanneonamissionrobinson

DAY 331 – VISION PROVISION

"Moreover, you are to take with you the silver and gold that the king and his advisers have freely given to the God of Israel, whose dwelling is in Jerusalem, Deliver to the God of Jerusalem all the articles entrusted to you for worship in the temple of your God." - Ezra 7:15-19 (NIV)

I had been asking God for a building to do ministry since 2009. It did not come to pass in the time frame I expected. I found my belief system was tainted by old traditions and values. I had to realize what I didn't ask God: to increase my belief and faith. To speak it into my now.

What traditions and limiting beliefs are holding you back from experiencing the flow of God?

_____

_____

_____

ABOUT THE AUTHOR

Roxanne Robinson
Atlanta, Georgia
Kgigroup471@gmail.com
Facebook - Roxanneonamissionrobinson

DAY 332 – ANOTHER LEVEL OF FAITH

> "The apostles said to the Lord, "Increase our faith!" He replied, "If you have faith as small as a mustard seed, you can say to this mulberry tree, 'Be uprooted and planted in the sea,' and it will obey you." Luke 17: 5

Growing up I learned God provides. So, I just waited on God, instead of setting up my money to grow. Until I was diagnosed with stage two breast cancer, I never thought about what I would do when my money ran out. I had to level up. God provides, but you have to give Him vessels to work with.

What vessels are in place for God to bless you through?

_____

_____

_____

ABOUT THE AUTHOR

Roxanne Robinson
Atlanta, Georgia
Kgigroup471@gmail.com
Facebook - Roxanneonamissionrobinson

DAY 333 – REALITY CHECK$

> "For by the grace given me I say to every one of you: Do not think of yourself more highly than you ought, but rather think of yourself with sober judgment, in accordance with the faith God has distributed to each of you." - Romans 12:3

After losing my six-figure income, my strategy had to change. Fast forward. I was introduced to a course, "My Money Emotions" taught by Dr. Sonya Hamm. I learned I needed to fix my relationship with money because it will either control us or work for us.

If your money matters are not going the way you like, you may need to reassess and revamp your relationship with money.

_____

_____

_____

ABOUT THE AUTHOR

Roxanne Robinson
Atlanta, Georgia
Kgigroup471@gmail.com
Facebook - Roxanneonamissionrobinson

DAY 334 — FEE-NOMENAL™ FINANCES PART 1

"They all gave out of their wealth; but she, out of her poverty, put in everything— all she had to live on." Mark 12:44

Let me introduce you to a 24-year-old married ambitious career woman. This talented young woman worked her way up the corporate ladder alongside her male counterparts. She received the most customer accommodations the company had ever received at any level throughout the entire company. Even more amazing that all her team members had customer commendations. She was known best for her ability to calm irate customers.

What are you best known for? Always be exceptional.

_____

_____

_____

ABOUT THE AUTHOR

Danielle Fee Vaughn is a founder of a nonprofit for single moms, real estate agent, speaker, mentor and author.
Danielle Fee Vaughn, CEO
Fresno, California
www.danikeys.org
dani@danikeys.org
@keys4needs
www.facebook.com/daniellefeevaughn

DAY 335 – FEE-NOMENAL™ FINANCES PART 2

"They all gave out of their wealth; but she, out of her poverty, put in everything—all she had to live on." Mark 12:44

The company created a new position for her with a pay increase. On October 10, 2001 everything in her world completely stopped. She gave birth to her second of three children, a 4lb/11oz daughter three months early. Learning her husband was unfaithful, she divorced, became unemployed with three children each with a different disability.

Now, she is a founder of a nonprofit and teaches single moms how to be FEE-Nomenal™ and create unique ways of income. I am so honored to tell you that "SHE" is "ME".

_____

_____

_____

ABOUT THE AUTHOR

Danielle Fee Vaughn is a founder of a nonprofit for single moms, real estate agent, speaker, mentor and author.
Danielle Fee Vaughn, CEO
Fresno, California
www.danikeys.org
dani@danikeys.org
@keys4needs
www.facebook.com/daniellefeevaughn

DAY 336 — DON'T GIVE UP NOW

"You can't seem to find an exit, a clear outlook, a clear vision. So you drive a further distance. Where's your turn? Did you miss it?" - Jay Anise (Excerpt from "Mind Gone")

You have not been left behind. You are not being looked over. God is preparing you for something greater. The things that you are lacking and the people that you are losing are all for a purpose. God's plan for your life is so much bigger than anything that you can ever imagine. Don't give up in this season. Daybreak is just beyond the darkest night.

_____

_____

_____

ABOUT THE AUTHOR

Jasmine "Jay Anise" Hendrix: Founder of Never Outta Ink, Best Selling Author, RN, Writer, Poet, Mother, and Servant of God.
Jay Anise
Birmingham, Alabama
www.neverouttaink.com
jayanise@neverouttaink.com
www.facebook.com/writerjayanise

DAY 337 – NO FAITH NO FEAR

"Has not my hand made all these things, and so they came into being?" declares the Lord. "These are the ones I look on with favor: those who are humble and contrite in spirit, and who tremble at my word." - Isaiah 66:2 (NIV)

Your next steps must include aligning yourself with women who are on the same journey. No Faith, no Favor. No strategy, no success. Take inventory of the five people closest to you in your circle. Do they have a Faith and wealth mindsets? Are they thriving or just surviving?

Yes, it is evident, it takes money honey. Your Faith coupled with Favor, and multiple streams of income will help you WIN.

_____

_____

_____

ABOUT THE AUTHOR

Roxanne Robinson
Atlanta, Georgia
Kgigroup471@gmail.com
Facebook – Roxanneonamissionrobinson

DAY 338 – FAITH IT UNTIL YOU MAKE IT!

"Faith is the substance of things hoped for, the evidence of things not seen." - Hebrews 11:1 (NKJV)

We are reminded in Hebrews 11:1, What is it that you are believing God for in your life? You have prayed and prayed and prayed some more and that "thing" has not manifested. Are you giving up? No. Even when you cannot see what you are hoping for, God is working behind the scenes to bring it to past. James 2:17 tells us, "So also, Faith by itself, if it does not have works, is dead." Are you putting in the work? You just continue to do the work and watch God! Faith it until you make it.

_____

_____

_____

ABOUT THE AUTHOR

Nikki W. Miller is an educator, entrepreneur, Christian life coach, speaker and author. Nikki serves in many ministries at Sycamore Hill Missionary Baptist Church and is an active member of Delta Sigma Theta Sorority, Inc.
Nikki W. Miller
Greenville, North Carolina
nikkiwmillerbiz@gmail.com
Facebook - Nikki Williams Miller

DAY 339 – MUSTARD SEED FAITH

He replied, "Because you have so little faith. Truly I tell you, if you have faith as small as a mustard seed, you can say to this mountain, 'Move from here to there,' and it will move. Nothing will be impossible for you." - Matthew 17:20 (NIV)

This powerful scripture reminds us that Jesus does not require us to have big faith, but "If you have faith as small as a mustard seed, you can say to this mountain, move from here to there, and it will move." Have you ever held a mustard seed in your hand? Mustard seeds are the small round seeds of various mustard plants. The seeds are usually about 1 to 2 millimeters. Now that is small. This analogy is so extraordinary because it shows that God does not require much from us. Your small becomes much when you place it into the Master's hands.

_____

_____

_____

ABOUT THE AUTHOR

Nikki W. Miller
Greenville, North Carolina
nikkiwmillerbiz@gmail.com
Facebook - Nikki Williams Miller

DAY 340 – INVESTING IN YOURSELF

"Investing in yourself is priceless. It is part of the infrastructure that helps to build your finances for a better tomorrow." - Lanee Smith

Jim Rohm said, "Income seldom exceeds personal development." Explore your options and write out your plan. What are you looking to do? Are you starting a business or are you looking to build for your retirement? Planning will lead you to the road of success, so write it down and make it happen!

_____

_____

_____

ABOUT THE AUTHOR

Lanee Smith is a magazine publisher and author who writes to inspire, empower and encourage women to become successful.
bayareamag@gmail.com
fb.me/laneeonline

DAY 341 – ARE YOU LIVING A LIFE OF CHUTES AND LADDERS?

"Failure is not the opposite of success. It is part of success." - Arianna Huffington

Having entrepreneur blood running through your veins is not always an easy way to live. It will be as if you are living in the game "chutes and ladders" where you work really hard to get where you think you need to go, only to spin and land on a "chute" that sends you plummeting backwards. It is all in how you handle those setbacks and the state of your mindset that determines if you will move forward. I began my company to help people stay on track, jump right over those "chutes" and have people making their way to the top before they know it. You are not on this journey alone.

_____

_____

_____

ABOUT THE AUTHOR

Tina Thatcher
Puzzle Consulting
To schedule an appointment: bit.ly/appointmentwithtina

DAY 342 – REDUCE DEPRESSION

"Creativity takes courage" - Henri Matisse

I bet you have a creative bone in your body somewhere. We all do. Whether it is painting, drawing, singing, writing, there is some sort of creativity that lives within you. Art in any form creates a magical outlet to reduce stress, encourages creative thinking, increases brain neuroplasticity, and allows your mind to be opened. Art also decreases negative emotions and increases positive ones. Studies have even shown that art reduces depression. Anyone can do art. I have used art as a creative outlet for many years. Now, it is a business that I love! We work with artist all over to show their work in our gallery, gaining them exposure and putting money in their pockets. What is your creative outlet?

_____

_____

_____

ABOUT THE AUTHOR

Tina Thatcher
Puzzle Consulting
TheArtCollaboration.com

DAY 343 – FAITH AND CANCER

"I Can and I Will" - Unknown

My mother battled cancer for seven years. She never gave up hope and she lived each and every day with love, inspiration, and purpose. The saying "I can and I will" was taped up for her to see - oh, how precious the sight was to see her add to that, "and I did". Her faith kept her going and her faith allowed her to let go. What is it about your faith that gives you a sense of peace to let go?

_____

_____

_____

ABOUT THE AUTHOR

Tina Thatcher
Puzzle Consulting
TheArtCollaboration.com

DAY 344 — WHERE DO YOUR CLIENTS LIVE

> "Don't be afraid to go outside the box! That is where innovative ideas live." -Tina Thatcher

Social media marketing is an everchanging piece of your business that must be nurtured so that your business grows. Your potential client "live" on social media, so you must show up on the platforms and speak to them in their language. We stay on top of what's hot with social media marketing and are always coming up with innovative ways to expand company's online reach and exceed their desired results.

_____

_____

_____

ABOUT THE AUTHOR

Tina Thatcher
Puzzle Consulting
TheArtCollaboration.com

DAY 345 – ARE YOU DETERMINED?

"God, grant me the serenity to accept the things I cannot change, courage to change the things I can, and wisdom to know the difference." - Reinhold Niebuhr

While you may feel like you cannot change the things you do not like about yourself, realize you can change more than you think. It takes time and determination. Is there something you have been holding on to that you would like to change? What steps can you take to make those changes or what steps can you take in accepting what you cannot change?

_____

_____

_____

ABOUT THE AUTHOR

Tina Thatcher
Puzzle Consulting
TheArtCollaboration.com

DAY 346 – FINDING YOUR PATH

"For I know the plans I have for you, declares the LORD, plans to prosper you and not to harm you, plans to give you hope and a future." – Jeremiah 29:11

We are all called to walk in the path God has for our lives. God promises that there is a purpose in all pain. You can allow pain to hold you back or allow it to give you freedom. In choosing how you deal with the pain in your life and what you take from those experiences, it can either weigh you down and control your life or you can rise above the pain, learn and experience what you need to so that you gain freedom from what you've learned. God's plan may be for you to even help someone else out because of the pain you have endured. What pain have you experienced that made you a better and stronger person?

_____

_____

_____

ABOUT THE AUTHOR

Tina Thatcher
Puzzle Consulting
TheArtCollaboration.com

DAY 347 – CAN YOU SEE WITH YOUR HEART

"Faith is seeing light with your heart when all your eyes see is darkness." - Unknown

Learning to lean on your faith in times of trials and tribulations will give you a sense of peace and direction This will help you arrive at where you are meant to be in life. How is your faith? Are you in daily prayer? What are you searching for?

_____

_____

_____

ABOUT THE AUTHOR

Tina Thatcher
Puzzle Consulting
TheArtCollaboration.com

DAY 348 – GOD'S PROVISION

"But seek ye first the kingdom of God, and his righteousness; and all these things shall be added unto you." - Matthew 6:33

Do you ever look at the success of others and wonder when your time will your come? Be encouraged by God's word. He tells us to diligently search for Him. We often lose focus of his commands and begin to look for ways to satisfy our own desires. Imagine being a hungry infant, that depends on its mother to provide nourishment. Do you crawl to the refrigerator or try to order take-out? No, that would not make sense. You cry until the milk is given. We are commanded to seek God's plans and his ways. All we need will be given. When we put our trust in him, he will provide all of our needs.

_____

_____

_____

ABOUT THE AUTHOR

Gaylin Munford is an educator, business woman, speaker and author. She helps women develop their God-given talents.
www.dayforaqueen.com
Jrosedestinations@yahoo.com
www.facebook.com/jenniferroseeventandtravelboutique/
Instagram:@jenniferroseeventdesign

DAY 349 – FAITH IN THE MIDST OF FEAR

"By faith Noah, being warned of God of things not seen as yet, moved with fear, prepared an ark to the saving of his house; by the which he condemned the world, and became heir of the righteousness which is by faith." - Hebrew 11:7 (KJV)

Noah was responding to God's instruction to build an ark. God gave Noah exactly what to do and provided the supplies to get the job done. Noah moved in fear and obeyed God's instructions despite the fact it had never rained before. Fear is an emotion that everyone encounters, but do not let it immobilize you. Have faith in the midst of fear, obey God, and move forward to build.

_____

_____

_____

ABOUT THE AUTHOR

Dr. Carol Y. Collum, a community educator and organizer, business consultant, mentor, and author who takes pride in empowering clients through leadership development training.
cycollum@gmail.com
www.facebook.com/drcarolcollum
www.LinkedIn.com/in/drcyc

DAY 350 — FAITH TO WIN THE BATTLE

"And Barak said unto her, If thou wilt go with me, then I will go: but if thou wilt not go with me, then I will not go." - Judges 4:8 (KJV)

Barak asked Deborah to fight with him in battle. Deborah agreed and stated with boldness the battle would be won and God would get the glory. Deborah's faith to win the battle was so strong that Barak was encouraged. Do you have soldiers of faith fighting by your side to help you succeed? Seek out others who not only have the faith to fight, but also the faith to win.

_____

_____

_____

ABOUT THE AUTHOR

Dr. Carol Y. Collum, a community educator and organizer, business consultant, mentor, and author who takes pride in empowering clients through leadership development training.
cycollum@gmail.com
www.facebook.com/drcarolcollum
www.LinkedIn.com/in/drcyc

DAY 351 – FAITH IN ACTION

"Go, gather together all the Jews that are present in Shushan, and fast ye for me, and neither eat nor drink three days, night or day: I also and my maidens will fast likewise; and so will I go in unto the king, which is not according to the law: and if I perish, I perish." - Esther 4:16 (KJV)

Esther had faith to approach the king to change a decree made to kill all the Jews, which could cost her her life. She decided to break the law and face death on behalf of her people. If we are hesitant to put our faith in action in the most critical times, we are ultimately putting the lives of others at risk. Esther's faith in action saved an entire nation.

_____

_____

_____

ABOUT THE AUTHOR

Dr. Carol Y. Collum, a community educator and organizer, business consultant, mentor, and author who takes pride in empowering clients through leadership development training.
cycollum@gmail.com
www.facebook.com/drcarolcollum
www.LinkedIn.com/in/drcyc

DAY 352 – MOUNTAIN-MOVING FAITH

"And Jesus said unto them, Because of your unbelief: for verily I say unto you, If ye have faith as a grain of mustard seed, ye shall say unto this mountain, Remove hence to yonder place; and it shall remove; and nothing shall be impossible unto you." - Matthew 17:20 (KJV)

Faith is the most important thing believers need and everyone has been given a measure of it. Without faith it is impossible to please God. When we have faith in God, we can overcome the mountains in our lives. Doubt and unbelief limit our ability to stand on God's promises that are revealed in his word. It is meant for us to experience the impossible through our faith in God.

_____

_____

_____

ABOUT THE AUTHOR

Dr. Carol Y. Collum, a community educator and organizer, business consultant, mentor, and author who takes pride in empowering clients through leadership development training.
cycollum@gmail.com
www.facebook.com/drcarolcollum
www.LinkedIn.com/in/drcyc

DAY 353 – RELEASING FOR FREEDOM'S SAKE

"Crying is a release of emotions, whether happy or sad, that allows you to be fully alive and present with your feelings." – Danyetta Najoli, *Tears to Triumph*

What do exhaling, opening your hands, and shedding a tear all have in common? They are simple, yet, powerful ways to release. When we release negative people, environments and situations from our lives, we begin the process of allowing something better to enter. In one of my signature coaching programs, Release, Allow, Attract, and Act©, release is the first step in order for the other three to take place with lasting effects.

_____

_____

_____

ABOUT THE AUTHOR

Author and personal coach, Danyetta operates a global growth & development practice. She serves on the spiritual growth and formation and racial reconciliation teams. Danyetta earned her degree in Business from Fisk University and is a member of Delta Sigma Theta Sorority, Inc.

L. Danyetta Najoli, M.A., CAP, Certified Personal Coach

www.Danyetta.com

info@danyetta.com

DAY 354 – DESIGNING THE GOD-GIVEN LIFE YOU DESIRE

> "I press toward the mark for the prize of the high calling of God in Christ Jesus."
> - Phil 3:14

Taking the time to design the kind of God-given life you desire takes prayer, time, commitment, and intention. When we are committed to living purpose – filled lives, we reach for excellence, despite the circumstances. There is a difference between perfection and having a spirit of excellence. We do not have to have it all together. We can place our trust in God and his process to refine us just like the refiner's fire processes precious metals. Let's walk like we are precious in God's sight while mastering excellence.

_____

_____

_____

ABOUT THE AUTHOR

L. Danyetta Najoli is the author of the ebook, Unstoppable Confidence: Sustaining a Posture for Success on Amazon.
L. Danyetta Najoli, M.A., CAP
Certified Personal Coach
www.Danyetta.com
info@danyetta.com

DAY 355 – I AM ENOUGH

"I will praise You, for I am fearfully and wonderfully made; Marvelous are Your works, And that my soul knows very well." - Psalm 139:14 (NKJV)

Your very existence exemplifies your worth, because God makes no mistakes. God is honorable because he created you out of love, wisdom, and power. Acknowledging that you are already enough includes loving yourself first, which positions you to receive, accept, and give love unconditionally. So, everyday look yourself in the mirror and say, "Others opinion of me no longer matter because, I am enough."

_____

_____

_____

ABOUT THE AUTHOR

Shameka is an overcomer that has written a novel of excellence that demonstrate how to receive and give love while not sacrificing self-respect.
Shameka J. Walker
Canton, Georgia
www.askshameka.com
info@askshameka.com
twitter.com/askshameka
instagram.com/askshameka
www.facebook.com/askshameka

DAY 356 – FREE TO LIVE THE LIFE I LOVE

"For I know the plans I have for you," declares the Lord, "plans to prosper you and not to harm you, plans to give you hope and a future." - Jeremiah 29:11 (NIV)

Don't allow the pains of your past to stop you from having a successful future. Years of sexual abuse and domestic violence didn't stop me from living the life God destined for me. The hurt ignited a passion of survival to help others move forward and live a life free of abuse. I encourage everyone to love unconditionally, live life to the fullest, and enjoy the freedom to be unapologetically happy.

_____

_____

_____

ABOUT THE AUTHOR

For more inspiration from me, look for my book 'Love Without Fear' at www.askshameka.com.
Shameka J. Walker
Canton, Georgia
www.askshameka.com
info@askshameka.com
twitter.com/askshameka
instagram.com/askshameka
www.facebook.com/askshameka

DAY 357 — WALK BY FAITH THROUGH ASCENDING

"Faith is the substance of things hoped for, the evidence of things not seen." - Hebrews 11:1

I have been married for almost ten years and now to be getting a divorce making me a single mother. I must ascend. No matter what challenges exists, you have to find your inspiration. My children are my inspiration. Ascend and dream big! Never give up on your dreams! Ascending is an important act because giving up is never an option. Rising and thriving is what will keep you going, knowing that God will never give up on you. Believe in yourself, because I do.

_____

_____

_____

ABOUT THE AUTHOR

Toni Rochelle is a mother, talk show host, model, and actress who empowers women to keep ascending.
tonirochelleuknow@yahoo.com
Facebook - Tonirochelle7
Instagram - Prettytoni7

DAY 358 – FAITH, FAMILY, FRIENDS

"Lean not on your own understanding." - Proverbs 3:5-6

The trials of life are often overwhelming. You are a good person and you are living life right in God's eyes. So, why does it feel like you are being punished? It is normal to question the divine because you do not understand the beauty of the path before you. I am here to tell you, stay the course. Surround yourself with friends and family who bring you love, joy, positivity and happiness. You are being made strong and resilient. Shine on and shine bright!

_____

_____

_____

ABOUT THE AUTHOR

Terrianne Lord Small is an entrepreneur, humanitarian, coach, published author and speaker. She has been featured as a guest judge on the MTV hit series MADE, starred in a local Baltimore Orioles Commercial, and served as a guest speaker on five syndicated radio shows.
Terrianne Lord
Gaithersburg, MD
Facebook - Terrianne Lord
twitter@TerrianneLord

DAY 359 – FREE TO BE!

"Lean not on your own understanding." - Proverbs 3:5-6

Excessive debt makes you a slave to the lender, you are never financially free. Focus on a simple plan - pay cash for your basic items (clothes, shoes, food and trips). Adopt a mentality of saving, if you cannot buy the item with cash, you simply cannot afford it. Use this simple principle and watch your personal wealth increase. It is your divine right to prosper, to be rich beyond measure and to be free.

_____

_____

_____

ABOUT THE AUTHOR

Terrianne Lord Small is an entrepreneur, humanitarian, coach, published author and speaker. She has been featured as a guest judge on the MTV hit series MADE, starred in a local Baltimore Orioles Commercial, and served as a guest speaker on five syndicated radio shows.
Terrianne Lord
Gaithersburg, MD
Facebook - Terrianne Lord
twitter@TerrianneLord

DAY 360 – DEEP FAITH

"Run now, I pray thee, to meet her, and say to her, Is it well with thee?" - 2 Kings 4-26

By faith it shall be well, so then faith cometh by hearing, and hearing by the word of God. What is the greatest wish you ask of God? What is the deepest longing of your soul. What about the things you believe you were put on earth to do? In desperation, this woman I have prayed and asked God for a child for many years and it was granted. Keep believing. Your answer is on the way.

_____

_____

_____

ABOUT THE AUTHOR

Carrie A. Williams is a wife, mother, evangelist, business owner, author and Elect Lady of Labor of Love Apostolic Church.
Carrie Williams
Chicago, Illinois
https://www.facebook.com/carrie.williams.10485546

DAY 361 – CREATE ROOM TO EXPERIENCE THE GLORY

"And when they had entered , they went up into the upper room. – Acts:1-13-14

Mrs. Shunammite was rich woman, a good cook and loved to serve to serve. Her sumptious bread had Elisha the holy man of God coming back. She took advantage of having an anointed prophets love for her hospitality and created a special room for him.

With permission from her husband they built an upper room. Have you created a special place for God to dwell? You can have the Pentecost experience, the Holt Ghost experience daily in your home.

_____

_____

_____

ABOUT THE AUTHOR

Carrie A. Williams is a wife, mother, evangelist, business owner, author and Elect Lady of Labor of Love Apostolic Church.
Carrie Williams
Chicago, Illinois
https://www.facebook.com/carrie.williams.10485546

DAY 362 – LIFE IN THE SPIRIT

"And whosoever shall give to drink unto one of thee little ones a cup of cold water only in the name of a disciple , verily I say unto you, he shall in no wise lose his reward." - Matthew 10:42

After being in prayer Elisha he called for shunammite woman, and asked what can I do for you? You have been too kind. Can I speak on your behalf to the King, commander of the army?" "No, sir" she replied. "I'm well among my own people." His servant told him she had no children, Elisha said, "This time next season thou shall embrace a son." Life in the spirit means believing that which seems impossible. Believe that God is about to birth something through you.

_____

_____

_____

ABOUT THE AUTHOR

Carrie A. Williams is a wife, mother, evangelist, business owner, author and Elect Lady of Labor of Love Apostolic Church.
Carrie Williams
Chicago, Illinois
https://www.facebook.com/carrie.williams.10485546

DAY 363 — FAITH IT IS

"But without faith it is impossible to please him : for he that comets to God must believe that he is , and that he is a rewarded of them that diligently seek him. - Hebrews 11:6

If you have never taken this step of faith, remember faith is not something you wait for like a piece of mail. faith is something you step out on like a bridge. Jesus paid the penalty for our sins by dying on the cross. He rose from the dead and is now preparing a place for those who put their faith in him. Walk in your purpose and continue to claim all the promises He has for His children.

_____

_____

_____

ABOUT THE AUTHOR

Carrie A. Williams is a wife, mother, evangelist, business owner, author and Elect Lady of Labor of Love Apostolic Church.
Carrie Williams
Chicago, Illinois
https://www.facebook.com/carrie.williams.10485546

DAY 364 – PRAYER AND FAITH

"Be careful not nothing; but in everything by prayer and supplication with thanksgiving let your requests be made known unto God." - Philippians 4:6

Sometimes, we find ourselves not going in the direction God intended for us. Through prayer, faith, thanksgiving and the Word, God will direct us and bring us into our destiny. God is taking us into a place greater than we imagined. He can and will make a way. With God's guidance, help and direction is available to us, but we must pray in faith for what He has for us.

_____

_____

_____

ABOUT THE AUTHOR

New Love Ministries President, public inspirational speaker, transformational leader, power speaker, helps churches, singer, author, have miracle services and conferences.
Min. Dr. Fay Williams | Liberty, Texas

DAY 365 — FAITH

"But the just shall live by his faith." - Habakkuk 2:4

F=Increases your ability to triumph over failure
Habakkuk 2:4

A= Anointed for total submission to God's commandments
Psalm 34:8

I= Increased intercession for others that their faith may be renewed
Mark 11:24

T=Temptation not received; defeated at the God's altar
Ephesians 6:16

H=Heavens flood gates opened pouring supernatural healings blessing and favor
Matthew 8:13

_____
_____
_____

ABOUT THE AUTHOR

Eleanor McDonald is a motivational speaker, author, and minister in Dallas, Texas.
eleanormcdonald39@yahoo.com
https://www.facebook.com/eleanor.mcdonald.94

IT TAKES MONEY HONEY CO-AUTHORS

Dr. Stephanie Adams

Dr. Sheila Anderson

Jasmine "Jay" Anise

Dahlia Ashford

Omotayo Banjo

Wanda Barkley

Greta Ann Belasco Murray

Renata Belgrave

Janice Berkenheger

Jennifer Biggins

Angela Billups

Sandra Beverly Blushings

Dr. Nicole Bramwell

Cheryl Bryant

Treneta Bowden

Dr. Kelly Bullock Daugherty

Melanie Campbell

Kristen "Minovet" Childs

Aida Cirino-Lee

Julie Clockston

Dr. Carol Y. Collum

Dr. Amy Cook

Dr. Johni Cruse Craig

Stacie L. Daniel

Kimberly Domke

Kim Edwards-Hatch

Charlie Fairchild

Jewell Fairweather

Tina M. Fernandez

Kentra FuQua

Rose Hall

Chou Hallegra

Dr. Christine Handy

Erica Hicks

Dominicia Hill

Stephanie L. Hutton

Chinita Irby

Velma Jackson-Wilkins

Doxie Jelks

Barbara Johnson

Dr. Roxanne Johnson

Shelley Johnson

Susan Jones

Pat Knauer

Rocherr Landrum-Johnson

Chimerre Lawrence

Rachel Leigh

Tarasha Lloyd

Terrianne Lord

April Mack-Williams

Pamela Mantey

Laurie Marks Vincent

Dena McCombs

Eleanor McDonald

Kimberly Mcfarlane

Kim McMillian

Victoria Melhado-Daley

Phillis Menschner

Jaresha Moore

Luz Morales

Annette Gayle

Ella Glasgow

Marla Godette

Jacqueline Goodwin

Catherine Green

Lavette Gulley

Yasna Guneysu

Tashawna Otabil

Rachel Parrish

Cintia Pedone

Shawnee Penkacik

Sonja R. Pickett

Deidra Pittman

Alandes Powell

Sabrina Protic

Kimberly Purnell

Jerri Reed-Taylor

Dr. Lya Redmond

Tracy Rickard

Michelle Redd-Latimer

Claudette A. Robinson

Roxanne Robinson

Toni Rochelle

Alisha Rojas Harrison

LeAnne Salazar Montoya

Dr. Soraya Sawicki

Michelle "Bunny" Scoggins

Myron Scott

Patricia Scott

Mary ScullyD

Dr. Carol J. Sherman

Erika Simmons

Dr. Nayshon T. Mosley

Gaylin Munford

L. Danyetta Najoli

Dr. Michelle Nelson

ShaNita Nolan

Tartanita Nowell

Kim Oglesby

Candace Wilkerson

Carrie Williams

Min. Dr. Fay Williams

Sheila Willis

Tywauna Wilson

Janet "Michelle" Wood

Tammy Workman-Lopez

Teresa Wright Johnson

Miriam M. Wright

Jennifer Yon

Samantha Simpson

Lanee Smith

Odett Stanley-Brown

Dr. Tabatha M. W. Spurlock

Chantel Tavares

Tina Thatcher

Lolita Thomas

Cindy Timmins

Danielle Fee Vaughn

Shameka J. Walker

Annette Watson-Johnson

Mary Webster Moore

Karin C. Weiri

Minesha White

FOR MORE BOOKS, CONTENT AND PROGRAMS BY PAMELA MANTEY

www.ittakesmoneyhoney.com

www.glownetwork.org

OTHER BOOKS ON AMAZON:

Fulfilled - Five Secrets to Achieve Your Dreams

www.amazon.com/Fulfilled-Five-Secrets-Achieve-Dreams-ebook/dp/B00DCHB6C4/

43847444R00215

Made in the USA
Middletown, DE
03 May 2019